STRIP NAKED AND RE-DRESS WITH HAPPINESS

How to survive and thrive through personal challenge

by Maria Hocking

First published in Great Britain by Practical Inspiration
Publishing, 2017
© Maria Hocking, 2017
The moral rights of the author have been asserted

ISBN (print): 978-1-910056-44-8
ISBN (ebook): 978-1-910056-45-5

Practical Inspiration
PUBLISHING

PREFACE

Sitting here writing the preface for my book, I need to pinch myself. Is it real? Did I actually make it happen? It appears so. Three years ago I felt a strong desire to share my learnings. I wanted to share my story to help others.

I decided to start by focusing on the three major challenges that I had faced in my life. All I knew at the time was that I was happier, stronger, and very fulfilled as a result of them. But how did it happen?

I started by going back through my past, looking at old notebooks and diaries, and drawing on memories. I started writing, piecing my past life together, and realized there were certain things I had done that had created big changes. My biggest revelation was that I had unconsciously been using all of this knowledge within my coaching practice for years. I had just never fully acknowledged it.

I wrote continually. Morning, noon, and night. There were times when I thought I wasn't good enough. There were times when I thought I couldn't be an author because I didn't know enough. There were times when I decided to put the book 'on hold' because I didn't have enough hours in the day. And there were times when I decided it wasn't possible to be a writer, a mum, a wife, and a coach. But throughout all of those times, my soul continued to draw me back to the computer, and back to my notes. I would wake at 3am with spectacular words in my mind and toss and turn as I tried to fight the words and go back to sleep. I soon realised that it was far more productive to go with my night-time creativity and get up and write.

As I wrote hours would fly by, and a whole day or night would pass with the words flowing effortlessly from my fingertips. But I didn't get many whole days or nights to write so I wrote on trains, at airports, in local coffee shops, in my car, and in my bedroom. The more I wrote, the more I truly believed that this book could help people, a lot of people.

Little did I expect an additional – unexpected and life-changing – challenge to come along whilst writing, so the book had to adapt to encompass it. Yet we managed to find many gifts within this experience also, which are laid out in the final chapter.

I want you to know, that no matter what happens to you, you can survive. And through adversity is the opportunity to thrive. I know for a fact that life may not turn out as you would expect. But it can turn out even better. I know because I have survived and thrived myself, and I've helped countless numbers of people do the same. My passion is to help people change their lives with my heart and my words, through coaching, speaking, training, or writing.

I know that you can live an exceptional life. And that you deserve it. I know that you are capable of far more than you realise. I know that you are a beautiful person, with many unique and special gifts. I know that right now, you may not be aware of these gifts, but I do know that adversity will help you to find them.

This book will help. I share my story alongside 'changing room tips', which will show you and guide you to a higher happiness.

I have also provided some free downloads to help you on my web-site: www.mariahocking.com. You can print out your 'Changing Room Checklist' as a reminder and access other helpful resources. Additionally, I recommend signing up for my inspirational newsletter so that my words continue to feed your soul. (This also ensures that you will always be among the first to know about my upcoming events and workshops.)

I lay my life, my learnings, and my passion for change throughout the pages of the book. I encourage you to read, relax, and share your experience with others. When you share your knowledge with those who need it, your knowledge becomes deeply embedded until it becomes a part of who you are and how you live. Happiness becomes your default setting, as it was at your birth.

Enjoy my words, and thrive on my learnings. I would love to hear about the changes that you make as a result, so please feel free to contact me via my web-site: www.mariahocking.com.

TABLE OF CONTENTS

INTRODUCTION

Adversity doesn't break you, it makes you.

I am an experienced stripper. I'm proud to say these words out loud.

My first encounter with true nakedness began at the age of 24, when all of my hair, eyebrows, and eyelashes fell out within just a few weeks. I was left devastated, and everything that I believed about myself just disappeared, leaving me feeling lost and numb, without a clue to my purpose or my being. I eventually found the tools to re-dress by digging deep and finding my inner strength, and soon realised that my nakedness, although challenging, was a wonderful opportunity and a gift. Having been stripped back to nothingness I was able to hear the whispers of my soul, which I had probably ignored for years. I began to create the life that I really wanted, and began living from my heart.

Following my experience, I found myself *living high and with purpose* and I learnt to give adversity meaning. Life became so intensely rewarding, and I felt truly indestructible. I lived what I loved and believed nothing could ever take that away. It wasn't possible to lose the light in darkness ever again, because I had been through so much, and I felt so strong. Little did I expect the challenges that came my way in the following years, all of

1

which have proved to be solid foundations for this book and its message:

GETTING NAKED IS ABOUT LOSING YOURSELF TO FIND YOURSELF.

Getting naked is scary. We go through life believing we know who we are and how to live. Personal challenge can slowly creep up, causing us to question our reality, inducing stress and anxiety, or it can happen instantaneously and leave us deep in shock. Either way, we may try to cling on to the threads of who we think we are, as we try to remain who we think we should be. We may try to avoid the nakedness we fear at all costs, but the battle is often exhausting. Trying to be the same person once you have experienced extreme emotional challenge is impossible. But what is possible is becoming an even better person, living a more fulfilling life.

The truth is, life isn't plain sailing, and it never will be. Adversity will occur, as will tears and heartbreak. You can't always choose what happens to you, but you do have the freedom to choose how you deal with it.

It's inevitable that when you tumble to the ground in pieces, you will cry, feel hurt, torn or devastatingly broken. In this initial state, it's unlikely that you will be able to see clearly or make sense of your situation, and you need to allow yourself to pass through this stage; it shows that you have a heart and have normal human emotions. Giving yourself this time and accepting these feelings is important.

What is not normal however is to begin to 'live' in these feelings, believing that what you are experiencing is all that there is. It's acceptable to move to the house of hurt and pain for a short while, but it's not acceptable to lock yourself in and throw away the key.

The key to happiness lies in accepting and embracing nakedness. It's about recognising that YOU WILL CHANGE as a result. Refusing to change keeps you in emotional pain. Life becomes about 'existing', rather than 'living'. The 'nudies' that triumph through adversity accept that they need to change. They don't know how, but they are willing to learn, and they seek ways to learn. This book is one of those ways.

We forget we were born to be happy. We forget we were born living from our hearts with limitless potential. As we grow and learn, we end up living lives influenced by others and their expectations. We move out of our hearts and live only from our heads. We disconnect from our spirits and our soul, believing that all we see is all that life has to offer. Those of us who get naked through adversity are the lucky ones. We get the wonderful opportunity to find out who we really are. We get the opportunity to move out of our heads, and back to our hearts. The naked people find their way back home.

My words, born of my own personal experiences, will show you how to use your difficulties to find out who you really are. Each chapter will take you a step closer to home. I've been to the changing room time and time again, and stepped out with a bigger smile on my face and more happiness in my heart every time. This book is your invitation to step into a space where you will be guided, inspired and supported by my words. My 'changing room tips' will help you to re-dress with happiness, and be who you truly deserve to be. I know, because I've lived every single word. I'm walking, talking proof.

I'm reminded of the quote:

> *"Do not go where the path may lead, go instead where there is no path and leave a trail."*
>
> Ralph Waldo Emerson

With regards to moving through personal challenge or adversity I'd like to ask you to totally obliterate those words. (No disrespect to Ralph Waldo Emerson.) Get a pen right now, and scribble through them in this book, I'm serious. Grab a pencil, or a pen, and do it right now. It's your first changing room tip.

Then find the brightest highlighter or coloured pen that you have and circle these words instead:

> *"Go where there is a path, and follow the trail."*

Why try to work it out by yourself? Why not learn from others who have found gifts and beautiful lives through adversity? In this book I lay out the path, and you will find that following the trail will help you with whatever challenge you may be facing. I invite you now to turn the pages and step into your journey.

You are now officially part of the 'nudie' club. Enjoy.

CHANGING ROOM THIS WAY

Before advancing, the 'soul' customer services department has a special message for you. They have requested that you read carefully with thought, and sign and date below to confirm your acknowledgement.

We would like to remind all customers that life is a truly beautiful and very special gift. Even with receipt of birth, we cannot accept exchanges or offer refunds, and we certainly do not give credit for years unused. In the event of you finding your gift unsatisfactory, we suggest that you visit the changing room as often as possible, to make all adjustments necessary.

I confirm that I will commit to making all adjustments necessary until I find myself truly happy with my gift.

Name... Date...

THE ONLY WAY
TO FIND TRUE
HAPPINESS IS TO
RISK GETTING NAKED
TO FIND OUT WHO
YOU REALLY ARE,
AND WHAT YOU ARE
TRULY CAPABLE OF
BEING.

GETTING NAKED – THE FIRST GIFT

In 1997 I got naked. Totally stripped bare, left vulnerable and exposed. Everything that I thought I was disappeared along with my hair within just a few short weeks. The only signs of the upcoming devastation had been two small, bald patches on my scalp, which revealed themselves in the bathroom mirror one morning.

I'd just given birth to my second child Brook, which delighted his two-year-old sister Jadine. Four weeks later, I began to get naked.

Juggling motherhood and waitressing in the evenings, I began to notice that my hair was thinning rapidly. Having read that this was very common after childbirth I wasn't too alarmed initially but then in the mirror I noticed the bald patches on my scalp; two shiny bald spots about the size of ten pence pieces. My stomach began churning as I tried to make sense of what I was seeing. I went to visit my doctor, who told me not to worry. He reassured me that it was very common for women to suffer with a little hair loss after giving birth. I left the surgery still feeling concerned, and I had every right to be. Over the next couple of weeks I began finding huge amounts of hair on my pillow upon waking in the mornings, and noticed masses of hair falling out while I was in the shower. I became consumed with fear and obsessed with feeling my scalp. Repeatedly my fingers explored the smooth skin, hoping for signs of re-growth, but the strange waxy-feeling bald patches stayed the same. What I was losing on my head was continually on my

9

mind. I checked my hair with mirrors repeatedly throughout the day. Every time I looked in the mirror I realised that my fear was justified: new bald patches every day, bald patches joining together, and endless amounts of hair creating their own carpet wherever I walked. Disbelief, anxiety, and crying quickly became part of my daily routine. The only break I got from my feelings and my thoughts was during the three evenings a week when I worked as a waitress in a local restaurant. Being so busy, I hardly had time to think about myself during these shifts as I gave the customers my full attention; this was short-lived however because my hair loss quickly became visibly apparent. I quit my job knowing that my hair would be falling into food. Besides, I was convinced that no one would want to eat in front of me, looking as repulsive as I did.

I returned to my GP, who tried convincing me that the hair loss was probably caused by my own hair pulling. Tears poured down my face as I whispered, "It's not." Inside I was silently screaming, "Please just help me." He prescribed a steroid solution to rub into my scalp but the hair continued to disappear.

My morning showers filled me with dread. I stood, closing my eyes tight so that I couldn't see the hair falling onto my body and then journeying to the plug hole. Yet I had no choice but to face that plug hole, day after day, because it kept getting blocked. Forcing the tweezers down, I would grasp the slippery loose clumps of hair that had become tightly entangled. I would tug and pull, hoping that I would only find a few strands, but the tweezers always came out covered in endless trails of repulsive, sticky hair that made me retch. I would stand and stare at my retrieval, looking in disbelief at what should have been part of me. My hair, on a mission, definitely decided that it had other places to go. The rest of it left me within the next couple of weeks, taking my eyebrows and eyelashes along for the ride.

One morning, looking in the mirror, I decided that my ugliness was enhanced by my seemingly untreatable skin condition vitiligo, which began in my teenage years. (I had battled with confidence over the years as my skin continually seemed to lose pigmentation, leaving me with large white patches all over my body and face.) Piebald and bald, I stood wondering why the tiny tuft of hair on the top of my scalp had decided to stay. As I stared at my reflection, I felt that I had been stripped of everything: my hair, my confidence, my identity, and my purpose. Being naked and exposed was terrifying. The world that I had once felt part of continued around me. I looked out of my bedroom window and noticed people driving and walking to work each day, going about their usual routine. I sent them silent screams from my head: "Don't you see what is happening to me?", but I didn't want them to see. I felt like an outcast: ugly, devastated, and hopelessly lost.

Returning once more to my GP, feeling totally numb, powerless, and barely able to speak, I watched as he wrote out a prescription for anti-depressants. Unable to fight my corner by this point, I left with the prescription and the words, "I'll try and get you an urgent appointment with the specialist," ringing in my ears. Emotional pain unlike anything I'd ever known had moved in and had come to stay. There seemed no way out. Every glance in the mirror made me feel even more distraught but I just couldn't stop looking, desperately hoping and praying for signs of re-growth. Eventually, I went to the chemist to pick up my prescribed tablets. Returning home with the medication in my hands, I had a gut feeling that this wasn't the answer.

Knowing no other way of helping myself at this time, the very next day I took my first anti-depressant. What I wasn't prepared for, was how much worse I felt having resorted to this medication only seconds after swallowing the first tablet. I didn't know much at this time, but what I did know was that every cell in my body and mind immediately screamed, "No, this isn't the way!" Feeling that I had made the wrong decision so strongly and unable to deal with it being in my body, I ran to the bathroom. I forced my fingers down my throat, retching to get rid of the tiny tablet that had caused such overwhelmingly toxic feelings. Whether it came back up or not I'm not sure, but I chose to believe that it wasn't in me. I walked straight to the kitchen and buried the rest of the medication deep in the bin so I would never, ever be tempted to go back.

Continuing to feel hopelessly lost, I sat sobbing and trembling on the sofa one day repeating the words, "Who am I? Why am I here?" over and over again. I hoped that the universe would notice my hysteria, take pity, and give me an answer. It never did. I was so confused, so scared, because I had lost me. I had been stripped back bare to absolute zero, whatever 'zero' was. I felt transparent, void of heart, spirit, and soul. My absolute lowest point was when a friend knocked at the front door. I hid below the letter box with my daughter, tears pouring down my face, and my finger on her lip 'shushing' her to be silently still. Hearing the friend walk away, I remember feeling as if I just didn't fit in my life anymore. Outcast from society, bald and bare, there was so little to grasp onto with regards to who I was, or who I was supposed to be. My soul had disappeared. "Is this what we experience when we die, when we head towards the pearly gates?" I wondered. Maybe I had already died and had become trapped on my way to the afterlife and nobody had thought to tell me.

All around me people continued to go about their daily lives, seemingly with purpose, totally oblivious. Little did they know about the woman who sat in her flat every day in 'nothingness', too ugly and afraid to step out.

CHANGING ROOM TIP
Choose To See Nakedness As A Gift

Years later, I smile as part of my purpose begins to emerge onto this paper, as words that you are about to read. My soul wants to speak with you right now, and it wants you to listen. As you listen, be strong, reach out with both hands and pull these words into your body, mind, and heart, allowing them a home in your life forever:

In life you will get lost. Stuff will happen that you don't expect and can't control. Nakedness isn't a choice, but how you deal with it is. Your future happiness depends on how you choose to see and use your challenge, and what you choose to find within it.

Ultimately, getting lost gives you the opportunity to find yourself. Everything trivial falls away as the truly important things in life make themselves known. False layers that don't really fit disappear and you get to find out who you really are. When you discover who you really are, you get to live the life that you really want. You get to live your truth.

Choose to reach deep inside and reconnect with who you REALLY are. Choose to see nakedness as a gift.

You can choose today to begin to see your nakedness as a space in which you start to become a research specialist, set on the discovery of the 'real you'. The real you is a person dressed with love and happiness, walking upon the earth lit up like the brightest star. The real you shines so radiantly that you dazzle others with your spirit and soul. The real you is a beacon of hope for other 'nudies' yet to start their journey. You just didn't know it until now.

Your gift is with you, just waiting to be unwrapped. Summon your strength to untie that big red bow, and take a peek inside. You are about to find out who you really are, and tap into your potential, your purpose, and your calling. Why wait?

THE SOUND OF SOLUTIONS

Oblivious to any gifts within my challenge at this time, I was a supremely miserable mum. My children put up with me spending most of my time indoors, unless I was feeling brave enough to 'run the gauntlet' in the supermarket, hood up, eyes down. Going out became increasingly difficult. People would try and act normally around me, but their body spoke a different message. They would start talking to me, but their eyes continually wandered to my scalp. It became obvious that many felt awkward and no one was ever brave enough to say, "What's happened to your hair?" I'm not sure I could have held it together if they had.

My relationship with my husband deteriorated, as I became paranoid, convinced that he was permanently looking at other women and their long, glossy locks. I remember a brave family trip to a supermarket. I was absolutely sure that he was looking at a woman standing next to the Rice Krispies, admiring her thick brown curls. As we left the store, my thoughts spilled as venom from my lips, and my husband looked in disbelief at the monster raging in front of him. Saturated with emotional pain, I watched him load the shopping into the car, and contemplated leaving him. (Looking back, my perception was obviously distorted. In reality men very often fail to recognise when their wife has been to the hairdressers, let along notice a hairstyle in the cereal aisle in a supermarket.) On reflection, I know that I probably tormented my husband with my comments and my outrageous behaviour. In reality, he was always there for me, and told me time and time again that he still loved me just as I was, but his words were wasted, falling on deaf ears.

In my mind, there was no possible way that he could love someone so repulsive. The only certainty in my life right then was that I was ugly and unattractive. I couldn't bear the thought of that being challenged. It was the only thing I knew to be true and I was livid that he wanted to take that away. Not a hope in hell, Mr Hocking.

My family and close friends were there for me throughout, but I just didn't have the confidence to be around people. It was easier to stay at home with my children, who loved me unconditionally. My young daughter never questioned my hair loss, she just accepted it. Shutting myself away with my children, I didn't have to talk about it. I stopped answering the phone and became an expert in hiding from people, and from life. The only relief I found was in solitude. Walking along the beach alone, with the soothing sounds of gentle waves lapping at the shore, gave me something that I needed, and that was certainty. The sand would always be there, as would the sea. Stepping into stability and what I knew was 'real' somehow gave me comfort. It gave me temporary relief from the negative thoughts. I would sit and gaze at the water tickling the cliffs on some days, and on others, crashing into them with a relentless force. I found comfort in the movement, and the taste of the salty spray on my lips; the very same salty spray that would once have tangled my hair. Somehow, being isolated and outdoors lessened the power of my negative thoughts and allowed me to feel a fragment of calm in my storm. My eyes often wandered to the cliffs that surrounded me in this solitude. How did they stay so strong? Some days I watched them being continuously pounded, yet they stood still and unchanged. I remember the ridiculousness of feeling 'cliff envy'. Were I to be hit by a wave, I was sure that I would just break into a million pieces and never be seen again. These thoughts would come to mind, and then just disappear. Thoughts on the beach seemed far less intrusive or permanent. Surrounded by the sights and sounds of natural beauty, my problems somehow seemed less important.

CHANGING ROOM TIP
Solitude = Soul In Tune

In my desperation and hopelessness, I tried seeking answers. I wanted someone else to come and show me the way, thinking that if I cried, wailed, and screamed enough, someone would eventually hear. They never did. Though I eventually managed to pass through this stage (as you'll discover), the real secret to being heard was eventually unveiled to me on a camping trip with my family a couple of years later.

It was midsummer, and we were visiting a beautiful family campsite. Surrounding the campsite itself was a large wood with huge fir trees in which play equipment such as zip wires, slides, and adventure courses had been built. There was also a safe and shallow lake, and in the middle of the lake was a huge wooden pirate ship.

Early one morning, we were informed that a small treasure chest had been hidden at the bottom of the lake. We were told that the first child to find it would be able to keep not only the chest, but the 'treasure' planted in it. An endless stream of children raced down to the lake, the brave ones in just their costumes, the more sensible ones wearing wetsuits. Sitting on a nearby bench, my friend and I watched as they threw themselves into the water whooping and screaming with delight. They began searching, each desperately wanting to be the winner. The water quickly turned opaque as the sediment was disturbed, and clumps of mud started to fly amongst the splashes. Intent on finding the treasure, they all searched with huge excitement and determination.

An hour later, the mist started to arrive and children began to get cold and despondently left the water, certain that no treasure had ever existed. My friend and I continued to sit and talk, lost in female conversation, watching the cold little bodies wrap themselves in towels before running back uphill, in the direction of the campsite.

It became quiet, and finding ourselves getting a little chilly and having been abandoned by our children, we stood up. Turning to pick up some wet clothes, I glanced across the now still, calm water, and noticed one remaining child, a small boy, standing in absolute stillness and peace. Captivated by his behaviour, I watched him turn his head, and slowly look around. He took a few steps forward, bent down and pulled up the chest.

Beaming with delight, he held his treasure to his heart, and scrambled out of the lake. Astounded, I approached the boy to congratulate him and questioned him as to how he found it, *when there had been so many children searching for so long. He looked up at me through bright blue eyes and simply said:*

"I would never have found it because the water was all churned up with mud. I thought that it would be best to stand still, and wait for the mud to settle. Then I thought that I may find the treasure."

Oblivious to the impact of his words, he picked up his towel and skipped happily away. I stood, reflecting on his explanation.

His words have remained in my heart, and I pray that they will in yours. With negative thoughts flooding our minds, distraught and in turmoil, we unknowingly disconnect from our soul and our answers. When we stop and create the space in which the 'dirt' can settle, we begin to see much more clearly. With transparency it's much easier to look within, connect with our souls, and find what we are looking for.

How do you begin to let your mud settle? How do you find your clear water? The best way is to take yourself into nature and seek solitude. Find a beautiful place that calms you and go there – alone. Let the only noises you hear be those created by nature. In solitude, your mind will quieten. This will give you relief from both anxiety and stress, enabling you to tune into your soul. Connecting with your soul creates a strong foundation on which you will stand and re-dress. Set aside even just a small amount of time each day to immerse yourself in nature. If you have many commitments, then use the 'edges of the day'. Why not:

1. *Set your alarm an hour earlier and find a space in which to absorb the beautiful sounds of the dawn chorus.*

2. *Find somewhere to enjoy a spectacular sunset, and know with certainty as the light disappears that it will soon return.*

3. *Find a way to spend time near water, beaches, lakes or rivers. The fluidity is positively reassuring and a reminder that everything moves. You are not as stuck as you think.*

4. *Embrace the sun, wind, and rain. A walk in the sun may be most appealing, but a blustery wind and catching raindrops on your tongue can be fun and invigorating!*

5. *Grab a sleeping bag, and lie out on a dark night for an hour and watch the stars. Observing the night sky is not only calming, but creates perspective. Realising how tiny you are in the whole universe will make your problems seem a little smaller.*

6. *Spend more time in the garden and make it a beautiful place to be. Sow seeds for growth. Notice that even though weeds appear to over-run the garden, each and every weed has its own beauty if you look close enough.*

Whatever you choose, know that what you feel during these moments is your 'default' setting; you were born to be at peace. All you need to do is to find your way back home, to who you were always meant to be. Sometimes we fear being alone with our thoughts, when being alone is what we really need. Only in moments of silence will you hear the messages from your heart.

"For me solitude is a necessity. It's where I can find solace and make sense of the world. The most powerful form of solitude is definitely in nature where the planet and its abundance can quieten the doubt and relieve the darkness. My most profound experience was when surrounded by lakes and mountains and I knew that somehow, something had shifted. I felt like I was emerging from a cocoon, the cocoon being part of my old self, a shadow that was no longer needed, and that was left to be dissolved by the waters of the lake."

Deryan Gilbert

Use solitude to hear your heart and access its wisdom. Let everything else fall away, as your truths start to make themselves known. Your soul always holds the answers to self-healing and it wants you to sit in peace to hear your words. Only in solitude will you experience the sound of your solutions. Amongst the rustling of leaves and the sound of the sea, you will get what you need. Use nature to nurture and tune into your soul.

THE QUIETER YOU BECOME, THE MORE YOU ARE ABLE TO HEAR.

Rumi

WHAT HAPPENS TO YOU DOES NOT DEFINE YOU

Following my GP's referral, within a couple of weeks I received my appointment to see the specialist. Feeling a ray of hope and a tiny 'lightness' that I hadn't experienced for a long time, we drove to the hospital. Convincing myself that today I would get my cure, I thankfully accepted the invitation into the room of my healer. This hope soon evaporated into thin air to be replaced with heaviness as thick as the darkest cloud, as the specialist delivered the abrupt and very unexpected words: "Yes, you have alopecia. There's nothing we can do, your hair may grow back or it may not." He continued to pick through my scalp, assessing the situation. To have a man examining my head when I felt so ugly was utterly humiliating. He then, with no word of warning, informed me that wigs were available on the NHS. He took out his pen and wrote me a prescription for one. A wig? I sat frozen to the chair in disbelief and total shock. I had gone to the hospital expecting a magic wand and a new head of hair – and definitely not the acrylic variety. Even the word 'wig' was ridiculous. (Until that moment I didn't think it possible that I could sink any lower. It appeared that there was a level below rock bottom.)

I was told that I could either get a standard NHS wig from the hospital or I could use the voucher towards the cost of a wig 'from the market' in Truro, where the proprietor apparently had a good reputation for helping people just like me. I stood sobbing, wishing for the ground to open up and swallow me whole. Hysterically, I refused to leave the room, demanding the doctor explore other avenues. He simply looked at me as if I was an irritating inconvenience. My husband eventually dragged me out and convinced me to go to the market, reminding me that it seemed to be my only solution.

Reluctantly, I allowed him to drive me into the city. In my mind, I kept questioning why they would sell wigs for *people like me* in a market. We parked the car and headed over, and to my horror, came across the wig stall which actually wasn't just a wig stall: it appeared to sell fancy dress items too. I looked at the hair pieces in shock. It seemed that there was a lovely black and white Cruella-de-Vil number, an Elvis 'quiff', and various different brightly coloured afros. I wanted to run as fast as possible, as far as possible, as soon as possible, in the opposite direction. Unfortunately, the stallholder had already noticed us looking and asked if he could help. Rather than say, "Your wigs are shit and there is not a hope in hell of me putting one of those on my head," I remained silently stricken, frozen with horror as my husband explained that we had come with a prescription. All around me seemed to blur and I prayed to disappear. The stallholder looked at my husband with confusion on his face. He then looked at me and quietly and very discreetly whispered that we were in the wrong place. Phew bloody phew.

Feeling rather embarrassed, we eventually discovered the wig stall and a lovely lady called Therase, who was to become a rock for me over the next 14 years. Therase was obviously used to dealing with people 'just like me', and she didn't question or give me sympathy, which was refreshing. She made me feel normal. Therase was happy and upbeat and began showing me her wigs. I began to smile as I tried on a blonde bob, a long, wavy redhead, and a short brown crop. The stall itself was very exposed, and the only place to try them on was in full view in front of all of the people doing their shopping. But Therase's warmth and smile soon put me at ease, and her ability to swiftly replace one wig with another without revealing my bald head was impressive! The little glint in my husband's eye began to amuse me. It was beginning to dawn on him that he could have a redhead or a blonde any time he liked.

CHANGING ROOM TIP
Weaken The Glue And Remember You

Therase's straightforward and very helpful approach allowed me time to separate myself from my condition. For weeks I had been wrapped up in negative thoughts, so much so that it felt as if alopecia had enveloped my whole being, and not just my head. The feeling became so strong that I almost viewed myself as a bald head on legs, the rest of me disappearing into insignificance. Therase's upbeat 'here's where we are at, let's find a solution together' approach allowed me to disassociate from my condition and recognise that it wasn't part of me, just something that was happening to me.

It's very easy when going through personal challenge to let it permeate our identity. We seek sympathy, wanting others to feel our pain and understand. Repetitive sympathy and a 'poor you' approach however can act as glue, bonding us with our problems. The more glue, the stronger the bond which then strengthens the connection between our adversity and our identity. We feel as if the problem becomes part of who we are.

> *Understand right now that your challenges are not part of you, and they never will be. You will never be 'divorce', 'anxiety' or 'bereavement'. You will always be you, just experiencing divorce, anxiety or bereavement. Allow yourself to detach from your negative thoughts and loosen the glue by seeking a 'sympathy free' day or week. Spend time around people who can easily talk about other things, or those with a solution-focused approach. Remove yourself from sympathy as often as possible, so that you remind yourself that your adversity is not your identity. It's far easier to move through and leave it behind if we feel it's not part of who we are. Weaken the glue and remember you.*

I left with a long, mid-brown bob on my head, which felt weird, strange and itchy, but it looked a hell of a lot better than my egg head. For the first time in weeks, I wasn't too scared to walk out onto the streets. Realising within just a few minutes that the fringe was attempting to destroy the contact lenses in my eyes, I summoned up the courage to walk into a nearby hairdresser and explained the situation. The hairdresser looked a little flustered and did her best to cover up her pity. She smiled awkwardly and invited me to leave the wig to be trimmed so that I could pick it up later in the day. The thought of walking out onto the street bald again when I'd found some relief was unbearable, so we went elsewhere. Having a wig cut felt humiliating, and the silence in the salon suggested that a wig trim wasn't a frequent request; the staff seemed unsure of how to act or be around a wig wearer. I've never seen three hairdressers simultaneously grab long brushes and, with eyes down, start sweeping the floor. Trying to ignore their reaction,

I sat silently willing the hairdresser to stop tugging the wig with her comb. I couldn't bear the thought of it being pulled off. Minutes later, fringe trimmed and able to see, I stepped out once more. I became aware of a tiny lightness in my heart. I didn't feel like such a misfit.

(I am aware that this may seem indulgent and inappropriate. I know that 'what's on the inside is what counts', but it really did feel that as the roots of my hair disappeared, so did the roots of my identity. Previously, I'd thought that as long as you were happy inside, nothing else mattered, which in many ways is true. It's also true however that everything is interconnected. If having a cut and blow dry or getting your nails painted makes you feel good, then make it a regular treat! This is why you will find me at the nail salon every three weeks having my hands pampered. If it makes you feel good, do it. Just don't rely on it for permanent happiness!)

Over the next few days, I continued to spend a lot of time at home. I still felt crippled inside but I also felt a glimmer of hope; the darkness didn't seem quite so dark. I would stand and look at myself in the mirror, first with my wig on and then without, hoping for a sign, or an indication of *who I was*. I stared intensely, deep into my own eyes begging for a clue with a heavy heart, but to no avail.

One of my early wig-wearing days out in public involved taking my daughter to pre-school. I remember walking into the playground, trying to act normally but feeling as if I stuck out like a sore thumb. Trying to overcome these feelings, I made the effort to initiate conversations. Many just didn't know what to say, and found it easier to turn their back on me, rather than talk and have to look me in the eye. On many occasions,

I found myself isolated and alone. I tried convincing myself that I wasn't being ignored, and that it was all in my head, but deep down I knew: people felt awkward around me. My true friends soon made themselves known. They were the ones that continued to talk to me just like they always had, and treat me as they had always done, which was a huge relief. And on one particular day 'wig wearing in public' I met the 'amazing lady', a total stranger who approached me and told me that she thought my hair looked stunning. She said that she would love hair just like it. I didn't know this woman, I'd seen her only occasionally whilst walking through the school gates, but on that day she gave me two huge gifts. The first was a much-needed confidence boost, and the second was the gift of knowledge; the knowledge that just taking a few moments to compliment someone can literally change their day. (Have you ever been on the receiving end of an unexpected compliment? If so, you will understand.)

Shortly after this, one of my close friends invited me to a party at her house. At this time none of these friends had seen the new 'wig-wearing Maria'. To say that I was apprehensive of their reaction was an understatement. Summoning every ounce of courage, I knocked at my friend's door and as it opened, I found her husband staring at me curiously. Frozen on the spot, awaiting his reaction, I had no idea what was going through his mind on its way to his mouth. Seconds later he asked: "Who put the cauliflower on your head?" and we all burst out laughing. At that moment, I realised that I hadn't laughed for a long, long time. With all my friends together, I soon recognised that they had no problem at all with me wearing a wig. Yes, I was the butt of many jokes, which I welcomed because it meant they weren't feeling sorry for me. They even called it a wig-warming

28

party. That evening was a very welcome lift and I remember it fondly.

CHANGING ROOM TIP
Look For Laughter

Sometimes laughter really is the best medicine. Laughter relieves stress, forces anxiety to go take a hike, and is a very powerful drug. Unlike medication, it becomes effective within seconds, and immediately lowers stress hormones. As laughter moves in, stress and anxiety move out!

A deep belly laugh is an instant endorphin hit which will allow you to see your situation in a more optimistic and less challenging light. It will immediately disassociate you from negative feelings, giving you relief from emotional hurt and pain. Getting re-dressed with happiness involves gradually replacing the negative thoughts resulting in negative behaviours with positive thoughts and behaviours. Laughter can help break the cycle of negative feelings so it is a welcome interruption. It creates space in which positive thoughts can grow.

I relied on laughter on many occasions during my 16 years of wig wearing. I had to. There were several incidents when my wig suddenly flew or fell off. Once, whilst disassembling a large marquee at a public event surrounded by lots of people, a large bar fell down onto my head and dragged off the wig in front of my daughter's nine-year-old friend, who was totally unaware of my medical condition or my wig. He looked first at my head in disbelief then down at what looked like a cat that had been hit by a car lying on the grass. Completely flummoxed, as if he'd just been astounded by a magician, he finally spoke: "How the hell did that happen?" I faced a split-second choice: cry and run, or laugh. I picked up the wig, threw it back on my head, laughed, and then laughed some more. At least I was entertaining.

The most dramatic incident, which required the most laughter, was at Center Parcs with my two oldest children, who were about seven and five years old at the time. Whilst in the swimming pool, I watched my children whoop in delight as they belly skimmed down the rapids. Feeling compelled to join them in their fun, I first discreetly tightened the elastic on my wig. I then launched myself down the first flow of water, accompanied by my son and daughter. We sped around a bend, screaming and laughing, and having a whale of a time. My whale of a time soon turned into a wail from my lips as, leaving another bend, a wave of water engulfed me. Coughing and spluttering, all three of us landed in a whirlpool, circling each other at the centre of the rapids. And around us my wig was circling, a spike of hair sticking out of the water like a fin. Knowing that I didn't like to be seen without my wig, my children looked at my head horrified then proceeded to jump on my shoulders and push me under the water so that no one else would see me. I pushed up through and gasped for air, laughing hysterically, trying to convince my offspring that it was okay. My words fell on deaf ears, because together they jumped on me again, shouting to each other, hatching a plan to try to catch the wig, arms and legs flailing in all

What Happens To You Does Not Define You

directions. One of them eventually caught it, let me up for air and tried desperately to position it back onto my head. Barely able to breathe as I had just nearly drowned, but with tears of laughter pouring down my face, we made it as a team down to the end pool. My wig and I arrived as one, which spared the lifeguard the embarrassment of having to fish it out.

In times of despair or uncertainty, it can be challenging to find moments in which we can laugh. The great news, though, is that even forced laughter can bring benefits. Laughter Yoga for example (developed by an Indian doctor, Dr Madan Kataria) utilises this knowledge and is backed by scientific research that proves that the body cannot differentiate between real or fake laughter. Even fake laughter lowers the levels of stress hormones within the blood. Try it now. Laugh out loud for a few seconds. Notice how it makes you feel.

It can sometimes be initially difficult to consider a smile (let alone laughter) when we feel overwhelmed by circumstances, but I'm going to share with you a little secret. It's your next changing room tip. I'm going to ask you to **Mind The Gap**.

31

CHANGING ROOM TIP

Mind The Gap

In any given situation, you have a choice with regards to your reaction. Between an event occurring and your reaction there is a 'gap'.

Situation ⟶ *G.A.P* ⟶ *Reaction*

The gap may only be a second or two, but it's a gap and it's the space where you get to choose the outcome. In that moment, you can choose to seek blame and crawl back despondently to the home of misery and stagnate. Or you can choose to face the challenge and smile or laugh to override negative emotions and allow yourself a far more productive perspective of the situation.

Your changing room tip is to use your MIND to spot the GAP, or:

Genuine
Alternative
Perspective

There will be a Genuine Alternative Perspective in most situations, and there will be smiles and laughter waiting to be discovered. You can either moan about the weather or dance and laugh in the rain. It's a choice.

When you recognise the G.A.P, use it. Rather than reacting instantly, give yourself a little more time to think and make the right decision.

(I've had to find and use my G.A.P quite recently. I was recently diagnosed with the beginnings of a macular hole in my left eye, and reading, writing and typing have become more of a challenge. After throwing a spectacular hissy fit and a few tantrums and after insulting the universe for donating this to me, it came to my attention that I was missing my G.A.P. I decided to go back and look for it, and I found it. I apologised to the universe and decided that it was trying to challenge my sight to make me finish this book. Time is of the essence. (Hence I've booked myself into a local hotel for the night to write, write and write. Thank you, universe.)

I invite you to join me as a G.A.P spotter. Use your mind to find genuine alternative perspectives and find space for smiles and laughter. Laughter will light up your life, your spirit and every part of your soul. Turn the volume up on your smiles until they become laughter escaping from your lips.

> "I have not seen anyone dying of laughter, but I know millions who are dying because they are not laughing."
>
> Dr Madan Kataria

DON'T OPEN YOUR MOUTH TO PUT MEDICINE IN. OPEN YOUR MOUTH TO LET LAUGHTER OUT.

GRATITUDE IS YOUR GATEWAY

With a little practice Minding The Gaps, I learned to make better choices. As a result, laughter helped deflect much embarrassment and the upset that it would have caused. However, still struggling with confidence and my identity, I also cried a lot. Not because I was bald, but because I was lost. I spent a lot of time thinking about what was wrong with my life. I had frustration, anger, sadness, hopelessness, and self-pity on speed dial and was very self-indulgent with my thought choices. On the surface I could now fit into society with the help of my new false hair, but inside I still felt hopelessly disorientated.

"Mirror, mirror on the wall, who is Maria amongst them all?"

No answer.

Until one day.

Early one morning, I was standing in the kitchen at our home, gazing through the serving hatch into the dining room. I noticed my daughter Jadine playing with her brother Brook. She was gently pinging the baby bouncer, making him bounce up and down. This was making him laugh – deep contagious laughter that reflected pure unadulterated joy. The sound seemed to penetrate my heart, my soul and my being. In that split second, I felt an overwhelming and unfamiliar gratitude, which filled me with light from the top of my head to the tips of my toes. For the first time in a very long time, looking at my children, I focused on what I did have in my life, instead of what I had lost.

My body and mind surged with new hope. It was the day that I changed my mind and undoubtedly changed my life.

CHANGING ROOM TIP
Get Grateful

The day that I decided to focus on what I did have (beautiful children) instead of what I didn't have (hair) was without doubt the day that my life began to change. It was a spectacular lesson with regards to the art of gratitude and the power that this has. Gratitude gave me the gift of time, a few seconds in which I felt a spiritual hug as a wave of calm momentarily enveloped me from top to toe. In this moment of calm, the chatter in my head began to fade, allowing the gentle whispering from my soul to be heard. It was the first time that I knew that I needed to change 'me', not the situation. And I knew that I needed something else to fill my mind and think about. In my nakedness, I had nothing else to follow but my guiding light.

**Gratitude is the gateway to your soul,
and the answers that you seek.**

When we experience personal challenges, emotional turmoil, or adversity, it's natural to feel upset, frustrated, lost, or hopeless. Our thoughts become tangled, minds confused as we focus on what could have been, what we have lost, or could have had. This results in overwhelming feelings, particularly anxiety and stress. The more attention we give what has gone wrong, the bigger the problem grows in our mind. The more our mind fills with problems, the less space we have for the good stuff.

By changing your focus and practising the art of gratitude, you can give yourself the gift of calm, and time away from anxiety, stress, and fear. In this calm you will feel more relaxed and therefore more able to think clearly. You will be able to find solutions to help you through your challenges. This is my experience, but it is also backed up by research. Dr Robert A. Emmons of the University of California, Davis, and Dr Michael E. McCullough of the University of Miami are well known for their research on gratitude. Through controlled experimentation, they discovered that people who expressed and practised gratitude were more optimistic after just 10 weeks. They also discovered that these people exercised more, and had fewer visits to their doctors.[1]

Ask yourself right now:

- *What do I have in my life that is good?*
- *Who do I appreciate in my life?*
- *What are the small things that I am grateful for?*
- *What can I be grateful for today?*
- *What do I feel thinking about these things?*

---

[1] *Journal of Personality and Social Psychology,* 2003, Volume 84, No.2, p.377-389

You may be a beginner with regards to the art of gratitude but with a little practice, you can increase your happiness dramatically by working through these three levels:

Level 1 – Be a Self-Gratitude Specialist

Start to identify your own gratitude thoughts and record them regularly in a journal. Reflect back and tap into happiness when remembering those special moments. Begin at this level right now, by creating your own gratitude book. Keep it beside your bed, and before you go to sleep every night, write down at least five things that you are grateful for. Maybe you are grateful for a special friend? The flowers in your garden? A day of sunshine? Allow your pen to flow freely. The only rule is no repetition. Find new moments of gratitude every day.

Level 2 – Be a Gratitude Giver

Continue to carry out the practice at level 1, but start to show your gratitude to others through the use of words or writing. Choose to notice greatness in others (spectacular service in a restaurant, for example) and call or send a note to show your appreciation. Make or buy a small card and send it to a friend with a few heartfelt words. Feel the immense joy in making others feel good with genuine words from your heart. Sprinkle some magic in the form of gratitude at every opportunity, and you will not only light up lives, but light up the world.

Level 3 – Be a Gratitude Giant

Having progressed through levels 1 and 2, continue to practise the associated exercises.

Look for and find gifts in any situation. Use these gifts to help you through your personal challenges. A challenge can bring either despair or opportunity. Choose opportunity. The size of the problem does not reflect your ability to come through. Focus strongly on what you can control, not what you can't. Focus on what you have got, not what you haven't. You may start to notice that you can lift other people around you with your positive attitude, as you begin to infect others with your sunny disposition.

(A beautiful example of a gratitude giant is motivational speaker Nick Vujicic. Born with Phocomelia, a rare disorder characterised by the absence of arms and legs, Nick faced many mental and physical challenges in his youth. Eventually he found a huge gift within these challenges, and now presents motivational speeches worldwide, to help others find hope and meaning in life. I highly recommend his book, Life Without Limits.*)*

By rising through these three levels, you too will rise. Gratitude is the gateway to our soul, to our silence, and to our peace. If we think about what makes us happy, we allow positive thoughts into our minds. We create small moments of stillness and calm. In stillness and calm, we develop the ability to hear our hearts and the whispers of our soul. The truth is we always have the answers; we just need to stand still long enough to hear them.

In our nakedness and in our stillness we have to follow our intuition because it's the only thing that we have. Our intuition is a light guiding the way to our 'calling' in life; a gift waiting only to be discovered in our nakedness. Other people may try to help and guide us with their words only to find our mind seemingly impenetrable. But when we're stripped right back, our wisdom comes from our soul. It speaks louder than the voices of those around us. It doesn't need to penetrate our mind because it's already there.

As small children we listened to our 'inside words', and lived guided by our intuition. Watching a tiny child play is an incredibly valuable experience. Notice how their soul shines from their eyes as they do what makes them happy: playing with friends, doing things that make them feel good, relishing time outdoors rolling in grass or splashing in muddy puddles. Small children ask 'why' until they understand, refuse to do things that they don't enjoy, and live unashamedly from their hearts. Their soul, so bright, dazzles everyone around them with its presence. They accept nothing less than being truly alive.

As a young child, many years ago, I would visit my grandmother, and on countless occasions she would lovingly pinch my cheek with her soft, warm hand. "You're rich you are!" she'd say. Years later, following her passing I began to reflect on memories, and these words that she seemed so fond of. What did she mean by rich? As an adult with children of my own, I now know that being rich is about being truly alive, and seeing the world through the eyes of opportunity, possibility and love. It's about living as who we really are, unashamedly and proud.

Being rich is looking at life through open eyes and recognising that the relationships that you form are your greatest riches, and that your true wealth lies in that which you create.

Only a short time ago, I took my two-year-old nephew to a beautiful beach close by. After spending an hour trying to keep up with him rolling down the sand dunes, I decided it was time to go home. Walking back across the beach, he became captivated by a tiny stream that ran towards the sea. He squatted down beside it throwing tiny pieces of wood, or 'boats', into the water before watching them float away. After allowing him a little time to play, I tried encouraging him to start walking back to the car. He simply and very determinedly refused and continued to squat in his tiny bright red wellingtons, toes touching the stream. Two more attempts followed but to no avail, so I took the 'if you can't beat them join them' attitude, to figure out what he found so fascinating. Crouching beside him, I sat in stillness (just as he was) and allowed my gaze to wander to the water. It wasn't long at all before I joined Jack in his world and became completely transfixed not only by the rivulets of water passing us by, but by the beautiful silence, stillness and peace of doing absolutely nothing. My nephew, totally oblivious to my thoughts, taught me a very important lesson that day. And I was grateful.

The key to gratitude is to learn to live in the moment. Allow yourself time to be still and allow your attention to focus on what makes you smile. Focus on what makes you happy. Joy can be found in many thing such as tiny flowers, vibrant sunsets or the feeling of warm sand between your toes.

CHANGING ROOM TIP
Get Snap Happy

One of the most effective and rewarding ways to learn to live in the moment is to get snap happy. Literally. Find yourself a camera, and wander aimlessly in a place of natural beauty. Photography will give you respite from your internal worries, as you become receptive to the beauty that surrounds you. Plans or expectations will become irrelevant, as you allow yourself to just 'be'. Focusing a camera lens on the tiny petal of a buttercup or a butterfly at rest allows you to focus your attention, and you will be able to rest too. Photography will expand the way that you see, and what you see. Taking pictures allows space in your mind. With space, your mind can begin to see your circumstances in a new light. Allow yourself to snap and be happy.

"We can only be said to be alive in those moments when our hearts are conscious of our treasures."
Thornton Wilder

CHANGE YOUR
EXPECTATION FOR
APPRECIATION
AND YOUR WORLD
CHANGES INSTANTLY.

TONY ROBBINS

MOVING WITH MAGIC

In my moment of gratefulness, changes began to occur as if by magic. Seconds after my revelation my legs took me over to a rather crumpled edition of the Yellow Pages (yes, it still existed in those days). I flicked through, looking for a local college. It seemed to happen instantly without a thought. Was I in control? Was I out of control? What was happening to me? Confusion set aside, I called the college straight away, knowing that for me to find myself something needed to change. I sobbed into the hand-set as I spoke to the receptionist. I told her my story with tears pouring down my face, and snot leaking from my nose. I doubt that therapy was in her job description, but I didn't really give her much choice. Through sniffs and wails, I explained to her that I needed something new to focus on, other than myself. I told her that I thought that learning something new would give me that focus. What I had totally failed to do prior to this call was decide what I actually wanted to learn. When she asked, I didn't have a clue. I was lost, hopelessly lost. Sensing my confusion, the receptionist asked me one very specific question that opened the door to change a little wider:

"What have you always enjoyed doing?"

Giving myself a short time to sort my thoughts, my life flashed before my eyes. In a split second I recalled secondary school memories of blasting up the hockey pitch as team captain with a huge grin on my face. I remembered how good it felt to run, and to run a long way. Memories of swimming, football, and athletics came flooding back, in a moment of inspiration.

"Sport," I said immediately, "I've always enjoyed sport." I was informed that there was a fitness instructor course starting in two weeks. Knowing nothing else other than I was moving forwards, and praying that I had enough money in my depleted bank account, I booked onto the course there and then. Putting the phone back on the hook and taking a deep breath, I let out a sigh of relief. Sensing movement replacing stagnation, I became aware that a shift had occurred, but was unaware that I'd stepped deeply into the changing room.

CHANGING ROOM TIP
Use Magic To Move

When the word 'sport' shot from my mouth whilst I was speaking to the receptionist at the college, it was powered by joy. Joy creates movement because we are naturally drawn to move towards it. We experience many moments of joy as a child, but as we grow our joys can become less of a priority. Daily commitments seem to take our time, and we think we have less time to connect with what makes us happy. This isn't who we were meant to be. It's not who YOU were ever meant to be.

In 2000, I gave birth to my third child, Kian. A few short years later, on his arrival home from school one day, a beautiful gift was delivered to my kitchen worktop. It was a crumpled piece of paper apparently stuck to his lunch box with messy honey fingerprints. These were the words that overwhelmed me as I read them:

The Magic Box
By
Kian Hocking

I will put in the box
A deafening rev from a pit bike
The sweet sound of birds singing
The sound of a roaring go kart.

I will put in the box
The first spray of pure white snow
The second big bubble from a hot tub
The last slow step from my dog.

I will put in the box
The spiciest bit of a slice of pizza
The sweetest swallow of slow hunny
The milkiest melted cube of chocolate.

I will put in the box
The biggest puppy eyes staring at you
The smallest flame of deep red fire
The bluest wave rolling to the shore.

I will put in the box
The longest swing on an oak tree
The warmest summer night of the year
The freshest morning of camping.

I will drive in my box amazingly
I will sit in my box in pure white snow
I will play rugby in my box and score a match-winning try.

Feeling the power of his words, that had come from his soul, I was overwhelmed with emotion. Everything he loved to do, and be part of, laid out bare on the sticky piece of paper. My son, oblivious, picked up his rugby ball and raced out of the door. (If he ever gets lost in life, I will take great delight in handing him back his piece of paper!)

Immediately, I decided that I needed to start using this very simple but powerful process within my coaching practice. What an awesome fun way to help my clients move towards happiness by enabling them to reconnect with what they love to do and their joy!

I started prescribing 'Magic Boxes' for 'homework' between sessions, and took great delight in receiving their words on a regular basis via email. The power of magic boxes became clearly evident when I discovered this email in my inbox one morning:

"I took some time out to 'fill my magic box' last night and this morning I feel a tiny ray of hope that I haven't felt for a long time. My daughter's suicide left me feeling destitute and hopelessly lost, and I never, ever thought that I would be able to move forwards. I know that my daughter will never come back, and tears drop to my keyboard as I type these words. Last night, as I 'filled my box', it made me realise that though I will never see the beauty of my daughter ever again, I can still see and feel the beauty of all the things around me that I used to love, and probably still love. My magic box gave me more than direction, it gave me hope. Today I am going to go out and connect with some of the contents of my box: walk

along the beach with the wind in my hair, go for a coffee with a friend, dig out my easel and paint."

We, the 'nudies', are the lucky ones who stand or who have stood vulnerable, devastated, and broken. We, the 'nudies', are guided back to who we were always meant to be. We rediscover our joys because we have no choice but to look for them. We, the 'nudies', are gifted the keys to our happiness in the silent spaces to be found amongst the chaos of adversity. During these times, it becomes evident that life is so very unpredictable and so very short, and that we don't get many chances to live our dreams.

To move away from pain and towards happiness, you need to connect with your joy and surround yourself with things that make you happy. Magic creates momentum. I'd love you to feel the power of your 'Magic Box' and urge you to use the next pages to rediscover your forgotten pleasures. Here are some questions to help unleash your thoughts and creativity:

What did you always love to do as a child? What excites you?

What have you always been good at?

Where do you love being?

What did you spend most of your time doing when you were a young child?

What makes you feel as if you are plugged into life?

What did you always dream of being?

What are your happiest memories?

What gives you a warm glow inside?

What do you love to do so much, that you would pay to do it?

And why not make your Magic Box a multi sensory experience? Use these additional questions to help you tap into what you love:

What do you love to see?

What do you love to hear?

What do you love to feel?

What do you love to smell?

What do you love to taste?

Unveiling your magic will start to charge you with energy, fill your belly with fire, and increase your desire to fuel the flames.

Stand triumphantly naked, and start to feel the warmth of joy from within.

MY MAGIC BOX

In my magic box I would put:

AN UNFAMILIAR OUTFIT

Following my 'therapy session' with the college receptionist, and having connected with my magic, I found myself moving. The first day of the college course had arrived. My body took me to the car to begin my journey, in more ways than one. My hands shook and my body trembled. My stomach churned as I sat behind the wheel and turned the key. Feeling like I wasn't even in my body, I drove off trying not to think too much about my destination. Fifteen minutes later trying not to think hadn't helped: it was all I had thought about. I pulled into a lay-by because trying to drive while simultaneously focusing on all the reasons why I shouldn't attend the course became too much.

"I'm still ugly…" "My wig may fall off…" "Everyone will shun me…" "I'm not confident enough…" The list was endless and I was incredibly resourceful at imagining the worst possible outcome. (I appeared to be a genius at it.) I turned the car around to face the easier option: home. Slipping the car into gear, it dawned on me that moving forwards towards home would technically be moving me backwards towards misery and stagnation, and back to emotional pain. If I turned around and kept driving, there was a possibility of learning and growing, and dare I say it, changing.

CHANGING ROOM TIP

Pain + Pleasure = Power

With the right tools and knowledge to overcome these thoughts, we can gift ourselves freedom to step through our darkness and towards the light. This was a process that I pushed myself through at the time, without appreciating the thoughts or actions that allowed progress. Only years later did I become aware that there were certain things that I did to help me overcome my fears. I share these insights with my coaching clients on a regular basis, and I'm going to share them with you now.

In moments of fear, ask yourself the following questions:

What will happen if I do this?

What will happen if I don't?

(These thoughts raced through my head when I was parked in the lay-by deciding whether to go to the college for the first time or not! "What will happen if I don't do this?" I would simply be retreating to misery and stagnation. "What would happen if I do go?" I wasn't sure but it felt like I would be moving forwards to a better life.)

By asking myself these questions, I had unconsciously associated pain with going home, and pleasure with going to college. Are you familiar with Scrooge, the main character in Charles Dickens's A Christmas Carol? *If you've seen the film, you'll remember that at the beginning we see much evidence of his mean and cold behaviour. Do you recall his transformation and generosity and kindness at the end? What do you think was his catalyst for change?*

Scrooge was visited by three ghosts; let's call them 'life coaches in disguise'! They helped him associate so much pain to his behaviour that it became unbearably uncomfortable. Scrooge decided that it hurt too much to stay as he was, so decided to change. When pain becomes so great, we want to move away from it. Pain can be the catalyst for change. Pain will push you away from your current situation; pleasure will pull you towards the future.

Associate both pain and pleasure to your current situation to find the fuel for change!

Having given myself a heavy dose of pain/pleasure medicine, I turned the steering wheel and the car around yet again. The lorry driver beside me watched me with amusement. I made myself a promise to allow myself freedom from negative thoughts for the next 20 minutes, my strategy being that I would fill my mind with playing a unique game of solo 'I Spy'. I chose simply to turn my attention to noticing things along the way that I had never noticed before. Surely this would leave less space for negative thoughts in my head? I then decided to commit to simply driving to the college car park. "If I still don't feel able when I'm there, then I'll simply drive home," I told myself, attempting to convince myself that I was in control.

CHANGING ROOM TIP

Guide Your Mind

Do not think about what you don't want to think about because you will think about it.

My journey to college taught me that if we try not to think about something, it becomes all that we can think about! If I say to you right now, whatever you do, DO NOT THINK OF AN ELEPHANT. Whatever you do, do not bring to mind an elephant, with its flapping ears and trunk. My guess is that you will have brought to mind an elephant immediately, and that you will have been fighting to get rid of the image of the gentle giant in your mind.

If for example, you think, "I'm not going to feel anxious," your mind interprets the word 'anxious' as something that needs your attention, and wanting to do the absolute best for you, it encourages you to focus on it even more.

Your mind can be compared to a small, mischievous child. Unless you give it an appropriate focus, such as colouring in a picture, it will try to colour the walls! Your mind needs care and guidance just like the small child.

Give yourself freedom from negative thoughts by guiding your mind. Instead of trying not to think about fear, worry, or stress, focus your mind on all of the things that make you smile, feel happy, or feel grateful for just being alive.

Here are some examples:

Replace, "I'm trying not to worry today," with "Today I will focus on smiling as much as possible."

Instead of "I'm not going to feel anxious," use "I will seek ways to feel relaxed."

Rather than "I'm not going to be miserable today," say "I'm going to practise happiness."

It's all about changing your mind. And you can change your mind until the day you die. As long as you have blood and oxygen running through you, you can change. It has been scientifically proven that your brain is capable of a process called neuroplasticity. This means that your brain is able to change and adapt as a result of your experiences. Pre 1960s, it had generally been thought that by early adulthood the structure of the brain was set in stone, unable to change. Further research, proved this to be untrue. You CAN change.

This change doesn't happen overnight, but if you practise focusing on positive thoughts repeatedly, you will start to re-train your brain and create new thought pathways. Imagine walking through a field of very long grass for the very first time. It will initially be more challenging, as you need to lift your knees to step through it. The second time you pass, there will already be a faint path formed by your previous journey. The more often you walk that path, the wider it becomes and the easier it becomes to travel. New thought pathways are formed in exactly the same way.

> **Practise the art of focusing only on what you want to feel.**

Forty minutes later, having arrived in the car park, I sat amazed at all the trees and buildings I had 'spied' along the way that that I had never previously noticed. It wasn't long, however, before anxiety and perspiration returned. I felt as defeated as my deodorant. The 'Go Home' voice became louder, raging throughout my head. Deciding I had wasted far too much fuel and time to turn around, I silenced the voice with my footsteps as I stomped determinedly towards the college. My new bouncy trainers gave me greater elevation as I silently recited "Humpty Dumpty sat on a wall" over and over again. This left little space for the negative thoughts which seemed determined to make a home in my mind; a highly effective strategy which I still use to this day! Minutes later, the ominous closed gymnasium door came into sight. Shit. It's now or never. Resembling Wallace wearing The Wrong Trousers, legs dancing with fear, I moved one step forward and two steps back. This was it. Now. I knew that to change me, I needed to walk through that door, and step into a new beginning. Lifting my eyes from the floor, and taking a deep breath in, I stood as tall and as big as possible in my brand new black Adidas jogging bottoms with lime green stripes, matching vest, and my wig. My hands dripping with sweat, I opened the door and stepped into my new life. The words "Hi, I'm Maria... I have alopecia so I wear a wig" tumbled loudly and shakily from my lips. There, there you have it. My right up front, bang on, in ya' face, no holds barred truth. I'm not hiding any more.

CHANGING ROOM TIP
Use Your Body To Move Your Mind

Little did I know about the impact of my change in physiology standing in the college on that day. Years later, I learnt why it had been so valuable when I discovered the research of social psychologist Amy Cuddy on emotions, power, and nonverbal behaviour. Cuddy discovered that by standing in a powerful pose (a pose in which you take up more of your surrounding space, for example standing taller and wider) for only two minutes, you can decrease your cortisol levels (the hormone associated with stress) and increase your testosterone levels (the hormone associated with confidence and power)[2]. Bring to mind a huge male gorilla showing his dominance!

If you are feeling stressed, in a low mood, or anxious, then simply stand taller and wider. Look up, and fill as much space as you can with your body, because you will start to feel better! Yes, our negative thoughts affect our physiology and make us stoop, look down, and appear smaller, but it works the other way around too! The way that we hold our bodies will affect our minds, so take advantage of this today and practise standing powerfully.

My top tip is to download the Superman theme tune. Store it in your music library on your phone, so that it's with you

---

[2] A.J.C Cuddy, C.A. Wilmuth, and D.R. Carney, 'The Benefit of Power Posing Before a High-Stakes Social Evaluation', Harvard Business School Working Paper, no 13-027, September 2012

wherever you go. If you feel that you need to lose some stress and gain some confidence, simply take yourself to a quiet place. Play the music and stand like Superman; stand tall and strong! You will find a smile on your face and you will certainly feel more confident!

Following my stupendous entrance and expecting a tumbleweed silence, I awaited the awkward reaction. To my astonishment, it never happened. The other students showed curiosity and interest instead. They questioned me about my condition and I wasn't stuck for answers. I didn't know much at the time, but what I did know was *everything* about alopecia. I had become the queen of hair loss research. Oh yes. Nobody could possibly know more. Within just a few minutes the power of facing my fear, instead of hiding from it, became evident. A new feeling made itself known. Was it... Could it be empowerment? Whatever it was, it felt remarkably good. Quite bizarrely, amongst grapevines and knee lifts, the thing that got the biggest work-out that day was my face; my cheeks were aching from smiling. My zygomaticus major and orbicularis oculi muscles were back in use, having been neglected for quite some time. Using those muscles made me feel happy. This however was a different type of happiness, unlike I'd ever experienced. It seemed to have an unfamiliar and far greater depth.

CHANGING ROOM TIP

Face Your Fear

When faced with challenges, many of us will allow our worst fears to run wild as our mind tries to protect us from further hurt, pain, or embarrassment.

"What if I'm not confident/clever/brave enough?"

"What if it all goes wrong?"

"I could lose everything."

As human beings, we are hard wired to protect ourselves, and it is normal to feel uncertain or worried when faced with the challenge of stepping through fear. Understanding the truth about negative thoughts can enable you to 'tap into your power' and make decisions that will make you feel better.

Understand that:

1. *Everyone has negative thoughts at some point, and accepting that they are normal can bring huge relief.*

2. *The presence of negative thoughts does **not** have to influence our behaviour.*

3. *Every behaviour has a positive intention.*

When we try to make changes in our lives, it is very common to experience conflict within our minds. Have you had an experience where you almost feel that there are two voices within your head trying to pull you in opposite directions towards different behaviours?

It may feel as if part of you wants to change, but another part tries to hold you back. We can find ourselves in huge internal conflict, which results in stagnation instead of movement. It simply becomes too exhausting to continue to battle.

What we fail to understand however, is that both of these parts usually want us to be happy.

It's very likely that the part that's holding you back does so because it wants to stop you being hurt. It wants to keep you safe, and it wants to protect you. Protected you are safe, and safe you have the potential to be happier! So, in reality the two parts of you are actually on the same team. It may feel as if you are stuck in a tug-of-war, but it's time to drop the rope! There doesn't need to be a battle! There is no enemy! Understanding this is very, very important. It allows the two parts of our mind to come together as one. Fragmented we are weak. Whole we are powerful and undeniably strong. Embracing this knowledge is a step towards freedom. How will you apply this knowledge to your current situation?

CHANGING ROOM TIP

Small Steps Create Big Changes

If you feel fear with regards to committing to change, then simply take one step at a time. Set yourself mini goals. (My fear of attending college was so great, that I broke it down into tiny goals: getting in the car, getting to the lay-by, driving to the college, walking to the gym, stepping through the door, etc). When we achieve one goal, the sense of accomplishment will make the next step a little easier; each achievement will have a positive 'knock on effect'.

Change doesn't have to be the enormous monster that you perceive it to be. You probably became naked overnight, or in a very short space of time, so the truth is, you have been through the worst. All of this was meant to happen. You have been given an opportunity to change back into who you were in the beginning, to reconnect with your soul and your spirit. If all you have to do is change back into who you were meant to be, then surely it's easier to take steps towards 'you', and who you are at your essence, in your purest and most beautiful form?

Open your eyes today to the possibility of change and think about what you could start to do. Small steps not only move you forwards, but also begin to create room for your spirit to dance and your soul to shine through.

Put pen to paper and make a plan for the next seven days. Write down one small step that you could take each day that would move you forwards. Then take action. How good will you feel in a week when you have taken seven steps forward? And because you will feel good, it's likely that you will be inspired to take more action!

Not only will you create momentum, you will also create a record of progress. This will enable you to look back at your achievements and note your transitions. Only look back to appreciate your success!

Steps I Can Take In the Next 7 Days:

1.

2.

3.

4.

5.

6.

7.

MY MESSAGE TO FEAR

I WILL LISTEN TO YOU BUT NOT BE RULED BY YOU.

I WILL FEEL YOU BUT NOT BE HALTED BY YOU.

I WILL UNDERSTAND YOU BUT NOT ALWAYS AGREE WITH YOU.

I APPRECIATE YOU BUT WILL NOT BE STOPPED BY YOU.

I WILL STEP THROUGH YOU.

RE-DRESSING

During the following three months, I studied, I smiled, and I began to feel a warm glow within. Standing in front of a class as a student instructor, attempting to teach them all to grapevine to the left and shimmy to the right whilst trying to co-ordinate my arms without losing my wig, was pretty scary. I kind of figured that I'd faced my biggest fear by then. I passed the course with flying colours, and I'd stopped crying. The tears that had once run down my cheeks had been replaced with sweat. Why was I feeling so damn good? What had happened to make me feel so much better? The answer was obvious: deciding to accept my baldness rather than fight it had been a huge step in the right direction. Acceptance had given me a sense of peace, calm and a new state of being. In the right state, I was able to make better choices and better decisions. The battle that I had created in my mind was over and I felt a lot less pain. It also occurred to me that I had returned to doing what I loved most of all: sport. I had neglected doing what I loved for quite some time, and having it back in my life once more made me smile. Was it smiling that was making me glow from within, or was it the glow that was making me smile? There was no point in trying to figure it out. All that mattered was that I was starting to feel different. The uplifting and upbeat music that I listened to whilst trying to train and co-ordinate my body was also helping. Music had become my medicine. The 140-beats-per-minute, sweat-inducing powerful tunes filled me with elation as I bounced around the room. The playlists of slower cool-down tracks that comprised of beautiful soulful tunes seemed to do just that – fill my soul. My medicine didn't have to be measured out three times a day and there was no chance of an overdose. I could help myself to it whenever I wanted so I did, relentlessly and without shame. (For suggested 'medicinal music', see www.mariahocking.com.) Dosed up with stuff that made me better, the foetal positions on the sofa of the past were no more. I now stood on the sofa so that I could practise and watch myself co-ordinating wild aerobic-style arm movements in the mirror on the opposite wall. Throwing my limbs around felt rather good. Opening up my body and my mind was starting to feel truly liberating.

CHANGING ROOM TIP
Acceptance Is Power

Acceptance of your situation is power, so give up the fight. When you acknowledge a negative feeling without resisting it, it loses its strength and momentum. I'm reminded of the story of Gulliver's Travels. Gulliver found himself a giant in an unknown land, tied down to the ground by tiny frightened people. He became a prisoner with hundreds of pieces of rope heavily restricting him so that he was unable to move. He tried to fight his way out with little success, causing the little people to attack and hurt him. Fighting created pain. Only when Gulliver decided to give up the fight was he released and free to stand tall once more.

Compare yourself to Gulliver. Thoughts such as "This shouldn't have happened to me," or "I will never get over this," are the ropes that keep you down and unable to rise. Whilst writing this book, I asked a trusted colleague, Deanne Greenwood (an exceptional medical herbalist), to read a few chapters so that I could benefit from her feedback. I was humbled by her response, as she shared with me her own personal story:

"My partner and soul mate of fourteen years, and father of my two young children, died suddenly and unexpectedly. I struggled to understand why, and how I would ever cope without him. As I spiralled into a black hole of sadness and despair, I started to read self-help books, and took myself off to the Buddhist Centre in East London and learnt to meditate. The Mindfulness of Breathing. I remember driving home after one session and the sun suddenly came out, and the radio started playing a Johnny Nash song about rain and dark clouds disappearing, and being replaced with a bright sunshinin' day... I pulled over to the side of the road and cried. I got it. From then on I found it easier to live in the moment, and find that silver lining."

Accepting your situation will allow you to release the ropes that hold you down. It's not possible to blame the little people for your situation because they don't exist. You have tied yourself down with your thoughts. This means that you have the ability to release yourself, too. Please go back and read that last sentence again and again and then one more time after that. It's a gift from me to you. Read, absorb, learn, and stand within my learnings. Why try to find your own way home when the route already exists? Follow the route, and leave visible footprints so that others who come behind can learn from you too.

Having released the ropes that had once held me down, I found myself immersed in a weird kind of new happiness. I found myself beginning to use new words: 'distraught', 'miserable', and 'hopeless' had been replaced with words such as 'excited', 'happy', and 'awesome'. How did that happen? Reflecting on my progress, I came to the conclusion that the motivational quotes that I'd begun to display in my home were helping immensely. Everywhere I looked there were post it notes and positive words, constant reminders of happiness, inspiration and encouragement. Words were hugging me every day.

CHANGING ROOM TIP
Re-Dress With Resources

The people who find themselves naked as a result of adversity have certain things they do and say to help them re-dress. Over the years, I have worked with countless clients struggling to find their way through personal challenges. The stories and situations may have varied, but they all had one thing in common; they all did specific things that helped them through, the majority of which can be seen within the pages of this book. With the world at our fingertips via the internet, we have access to many incredibly inspiring stories and video clips from which we can learn. We don't have to spend years searching our soul trying to figure it all out alone.

Why not spend a little time each day using these resources? Find people who have experienced adversity and find out what they did to get through. Seek stories that both touch your heart and ignite your soul. I highly recommend www.TED.com. *Research inspiring quotes that resonate with you, print them out, and stick them around your home. If you are stuck for ideas, then, like me, decorate the back of your toilet door with words that make you feel alive. Sit on your throne and surround yourself with words fit for the greatness of a king! Surround yourself with the finery of optimism. This will impact not only you, but also the other beings that choose to use your bathroom. Just recently my eldest son yelled, "Mum, have you seen what Kian [his younger brother] has done to the back of the bathroom door?" Assuming this was a tell-tale situation, I walked to the door expecting to see my quotes altered in some graffiti-style, humorous way. Instead I found a picture of a tiny dog wearing a life jacket on a surfboard at sea accompanied by my son's creation:*

Life's like a beautiful wave
There's lots of up and downs
You can swim straight through them
Or you can go with the flow
All that matters is you get over them
Otherwise they may crash down upon you!

How wrong I had been to think that my boys were aggravating each other! My youngest was obviously proud of his words and his brother had been touched by them, too.

You are surrounded right now by a phenomenal amount of resources. Open your mind to allow your eyes to see them. Use people, books, and the World Wide Web to learn from the best! In the world of Neuro Linguistic Programming, this is known as a process called modelling. It means finding someone who has got what you want and finding out how they got it before implementing similar strategies yourself. There are many who have gone before you, and there will be many that come behind you. Become part of the path and deepen the trail. Step forwards and step up.

SEEKING SILVER LININGS

Having released the ropes that had been holding me down, it began to occur to me that I was beginning to discover not who I was before, but who I really wanted to be. With a strong desire building to explore this 'new' me and a desire to feed my passion, it became evident that reaching the 'middle ground' simply wasn't enough. I wanted more. I felt clothed with a growing confidence but still owned a sense of vulnerability, my destination still unclear.

Thoughts of teaching my own fitness classes niggled away at me constantly, causing overwhelming excitement. The fizziness almost made me believe that I had champagne running through my veins. These thoughts were constantly interrupted, however, by the little voice in my head that kept making itself known: *What if you are not good enough? What if your wig falls off when you are teaching? What if people laugh at you?*

Implementing strategies that I had learnt from previous experiences (standing tall, stomping loudly to silence the gremlins in my head, and only allowing positive thoughts into my mind), I approached the local sports centre. Knowing that there were no fitness classes currently running at the centre, I suggested that it may benefit the local community and the centre to promote them. I spotted a problem, found a solution and offered my services.

Without giving it a second thought, they agreed. A week later I showed up to teach aerobics in the only space available – the squash court. Waiting for participants to arrive for my first ever class, I felt incredibly vulnerable. I stood next to my brand new stereo, knees knocking and body trembling. My wig itched my scalp, and sweat trickled down my face, as I waited for people to come and wondered if anyone would turn up. Three did. When the hour was up, they left not only sweating but smiling, too. I collapsed in the corner, relieved, happy, and proud. My wig had remained on my head, and my confidence had been fuelled. Unfortunately, the squash court lived up to its name as my classes got busier. After some investigation, I decided that I would be better off in many ways if I became self-employed and set up my own business teaching in various locations, in bigger halls, in the community.

Setting up my own business involved slightly more creative thinking, and I knew I had to somehow let people know about my classes in order to make it successful. I toyed with many ideas, and tried figuring out how to brand my classes, and what made me unique. Struggling for inspiration I decided to go for a cycle. I bundled up my young son in layers and strapped him into a kiddie seat over the back wheel. I cycled out of the housing estate and along a small path overhung by trees. Being outside made me feel alive and with a beaming smile on my face, I pedalled hard to increase the exhilaration. My young son screamed with delight as wisps of his soft beautiful baby hair were tickled by the wind. I felt happy, free, and warm. A split second later, though, my head felt cold and naked. I turned back and saw the answer to my branding dilemma hanging in a tree.

Knowing with absolute certainty that I was the only wig-wearing fitness instructor around, I decided to write my own editorials for the local newspapers, and send them my story. It was definitely my unique selling point! They must have liked it because my words were published in many local newspapers the following week. It was huge promotion, which didn't cost me a penny! As my classes grew, so did my confidence and self-belief. Only a few weeks later, when somebody approached me to tell me that I had inspired them, did I fully acknowledge my transition. There hadn't been a self-pity moment for quite some time. The force that had ripped me naked had disappeared, leaving behind a new me, re-dressed with undeniable newfound confidence, invincible, and ready to take on the world!

Or so I thought...

CHANGING ROOM TIP
Spot The Silver

Utilising the force of the blow is about becoming a highly effective and expert 'silver lining' spotter. Does every situation have a silver lining? Absolutely, but only if you choose to look for it. Experience has taught me that sometimes people find it hard to even contemplate that there could be a silver lining in their devastation. Immense pain sometimes overshadows the thought of any possible silver, especially in the very early days of adversity. As time passes however, and with the right mind-set, clouds will definitely clear. This will allow you to find the light in your darkness.

I am reminded of an encounter with a gentleman at an airport. We were sitting in the departure lounge and began conversing as he noticed the title of the book that I was reading in which the word 'healing' appeared. He sat with a heaviness and sadness as he attempted a small smile and uttered the words, "I wish I could heal." (Isn't it strange the way that we seem to attract certain people into our lives?) He then proceeded to tell me that he had been struggling to come out of depression since his teenage son had been killed by a drunk driver five years earlier. My heart instantly went out to him and tears filled my eyes as I saw his nakedness and his sorrow. He talked and I listened, we connected, and he eventually smiled. Sensing an opportunity, I decided to share with him a story about a married couple I knew many years ago. This couple had been through something very similar, and lost two children in a car accident, through the fault of a drunk driver. I told him that they had felt exactly the same, but eventually they decided to seek something positive in the devastation. They eventually discovered that their only way forward was to give their tragedy meaning. They began to focus on educating people about the dangers of alcohol and driving, in the hope that it would prevent others from going through their experiences. As a result of this, other people who had lost young children in various ways also began to contact them. They went on to provide invaluable support to others struggling to deal with grief, and made many very deep and heartfelt relationships because of it. Sitting in the departure lounge next to a total stranger who had just opened his heart to me, and even through the sadness, I felt good. I felt good because I saw tears in his eyes, and in his tears, I saw hope.

There is always a positive in every situation, a strand of silver just waiting to be polished in order to shine. Losing my hair at the time was initially devastating, but hand on heart, I look back now and can say with great confidence that it was one of the best things that has ever happened to me. Had I not lost my hair, I would still be living a life designed by others. I would be meandering along, doing what I thought I should be doing instead of what I was meant to be doing during my time here on earth. It gave me the incredible and very rare opportunity to become one of the people who get completely and devastatingly lost, in order to discover their true gifts and who they really are.

In your life right now, there will be people that you know of that have found themselves. You may have mistaken them for naturally confident people, born into happy lives. Think of someone you know who lights up a room with their presence. Do you notice that they smile endlessly, making it impossible for others not to smile? Are you aware of their kind and compassionate nature, or their heartfelt and warm comments? People with these qualities have usually been to a very dark place, and worked hard to re-dress and find their light. Often these people have been through the toughest times. You just didn't know it until now.

One of my most powerful encounters with a re-dresser was upon meeting Aimee Stewart. I met Aimee on a training course in Scotland. Being a residential course, I started to make myself at home in the shared accommodation, and a few moments later was joined by another course participant.

Aimee introduced herself and we began talking and I found myself being immediately captivated by her positivity. Her soul seemed to shine radiantly through every pore, reflecting outstanding and genuine happiness. Later, whilst sat in the training room, I found myself noticing the impact that she had on the rest of the group participants; she bore the qualities of the brightest sunbeam, lighting up the room and dazzling others with her beautiful but humble presence. She is the closest thing that I have ever experienced to a human angel. I remember at the time wondering if Aimee had managed to get through life being untainted by experiences or others. Was it even possible? Or had she been through difficult times, and was living a higher life as a result? She just seemed so 'alive', owning and sharing the spirit and soul that we often see in that of a child. Aimee eventually shared her story and I feel privileged to include it within the pages of this book:

"I remember being 5 and my sister died suddenly. It made me realise from a very young age that life can change very quickly. It made me realise the impermanence of our reality and not only to cherish each moment but to tell our loved ones we love them, every day! It helped me not to take things for granted but her death also gave me a tremendous strength and resilience. She was the most amazing and beautiful gift. She will live on in the hearts of all who knew her and loved her forever. I remember being about 7 and having very deep thoughts about life and the reality we experience and I said to an adult: 'I think life is a dream and when we die we wake up.' I still think this! This helps me through the toughest of life's tests. It helps me to feel connected to life but not to take *it too seriously because we are here to live and enjoy it. Not to suffer. I guess my life's journey is teaching me to be me. Real, flawed and imperfect in all my glory with no apologies. If I get hurt or let down, or I lose someone close, or I fail, it's okay because it's part of life's gift and through the darkness comes a lot of light and connection with others."*

What positives could you draw from your current situation? What is the best thing about this happening to you? (If you struggle to find positives, then dig deeper.) Your silver shines brightly within, waiting patiently to be discovered. It will always be there but only becomes visible when you choose to look for it. Choose to look for it today by becoming a silver spotter. Give your shine permission to rise.

"The most beautiful people we have known are those who have known defeat, known suffering, known struggle, known loss, and have found their way out of the depths. These persons have an appreciation, a sensitivity, and an understanding of life that fills them with compassion, gentleness, and a deep loving concern. Beautiful people do not just happen."

Elisabeth Kübler-Ross

A

DEEP

VALUABLE

EXPERIENCE

REVEALING the

STRENGTH and

INTEGRITY of the

TRUE

YOU

BACK TO THE CHANGING ROOM – THE SECOND GIFT

Three years later, my career as a wig-wearing fitness instructor was flourishing. Following further training I found myself teaching a wide variety of classes. I became addicted to the euphoria of a spirit-feeding sweaty session and loved my work with my heart and soul. My family became used to my kitchen choreography sessions. They would frequently find me dancing in the kitchen with music blaring as I mashed the potatoes and chopped the carrots. By now, my wig took the form of a dark auburn crop, and my real hair occasionally sprouted back in tiny patches before falling out once more. My eyebrows and eyelashes were showing signs of re-growth; tiny baby, wispy hairs that would almost tease me by appearing then deciding to disappear yet again. At one point I tried wearing false eyelashes and drawing on eyebrows. The false lashes ended up in my cornflakes on more than one occasion. As my artistic skills have never been particularly great, my eyebrows resembled caterpillars that had been run over with a car. I decided that *au naturel* was a better look for me than 'drag queen', and my cornflakes tasted a lot better.

My confidence had grown remarkably, and my passion for my work seemed to possess every cell in my body. This passion unleashed had an amazing effect on my classes. Every session that I taught left me feeling alive and fully charged, so much so that I wanted to 'plug in' as often as possible. My classes were hi energy, hi impact and on fire and I loved every second.

I pushed my body to its limits and delighted in the after burn. Nothing would stop me teaching. Even when feeling a little under the weather, dance and sweat was my medicine. I was invincible and indestructible. Or was I? I began to feel a rising breeze. Never did I dream that the wind of change was about to appear once more and toss me back into the changing room.

Tiredness found its way into my life, then extreme tiredness, then exhaustion. Pushing through, I stood at the front of a dance fitness class that I was teaching in a small village hall with the intention of demonstrating an arm combination to the participants. One of the movements involved lifting my arms above my head and reaching high. Shock then panic set in, at the extreme heaviness and pain that I felt attempting this. It was my first real sign that all was not well. The physical exhaustion continued and additional symptoms appeared. My arm and leg muscles took on a life of their own in the evenings, visibly and uncontrollably twitching whenever I was at rest, to the point where I felt like I wasn't getting any rest. A visit to the doctor resulted in blood tests which came back normal, but I still had an underlying fear that something was really badly wrong with my body.

Becoming stressed and anxious, I began to felt isolated and alone. My symptoms continued but repeated doctors' appointments resulted in little help. They just couldn't find anything wrong. A brain scan was clear, and further blood tests again came back normal. I began to regularly feel as if heavy weights were pressing on my sternum and squashing my lungs. The solution became to take deeper and deeper breaths to overcome these feelings, which quickly developed into full-blown panic attacks that seemed to take over my mind and body. The doctor eventually prescribed medication to lessen the muscle twitching in my arms and legs. This did help but the extreme tiredness and weakness continued and worsened. I felt permanently totally exhausted, and frustrated. Unable to keep up with my life, and with my health declining further, I knew that letting go of my fitness classes was my only option. Endless tears revealed my true fear; yet again I felt like I was losing me. I had a sense of detachment from everything that had helped me re-build my life. After much thought, and with steely determination not to lose it all again, I decided to cling onto the thread of a relaxation class that I taught. Every week I showed up to that class, head held high. I smiled, and pretended that my life was amazing. I returned home afterwards barely able to walk, and went straight to bed. I didn't know what was wrong with me, but I did know that I was a fitness instructor and that I loved my job. It made me feel alive. I had to hold onto this with my life. It was the only hope that I had, and I struggled on.

At weekends, my husband and I would usually go out with the children for a muddy walk in our boots, a simple pleasure that brought much fun and joy to our lives. As my health deteriorated, it got to the stage where I would sit in the car and watch my family walk away without me. I just couldn't find the energy to accompany them and it broke my heart, so instead I would just sit and cry. On the occasions that I tried, I needed to sleep for a long time afterwards to recover. The panic attacks became more frequent, appearing three or four times a day, especially at school pick-up time which was very difficult. On some days I just couldn't get out of the car, and had to rely on friends to bring my children to me. Stepping out of the car triggered the crushing feeling in my chest and the fear of not being able to breathe. At home, housework became impossible due to the physical exhaustion. Cleaning windows and hanging out washing resulted in immense pain in my arm muscles. For most of the day I just did the bare minimum necessary to feed and clothe my children. (My housework skills are far from top notch, and have been the butt of friends' jokes for years, as the lovely magnets that cover my fridge demonstrate, but this really wasn't a tactic to avoid the vacuuming.)

The symptoms continued and I was totally convinced that I had something seriously wrong with me. Was it a brain tumour or some rare weird neurological disease? Thoughts like these flooded my mind on a daily basis. My doctor tried to be helpful but I could tell that he thought I was crazy. And at this time, if I'm honest, I was doubting my sanity too.

Until one day.

My husband at the time was working in the mobility industry, running his own business. He regularly came into contact with people with health issues. One day he began chatting with one of his customers about my condition. This particular lady, who suffered with Chronic Fatigue Syndrome, listened and remarked that my symptoms sounded very much like hers. She recommended that I return to my GP and ask to be referred to a specialist. She gave us the name of a man who specialised in working with people suffering from this condition. Being sceptical, I told her that I had never really believed that there was such a thing as Chronic Fatigue Syndrome, and I therefore knew very little about it but I was desperate for help. A few weeks later, I found myself at an appointment with the suggested specialist. I poured out my heart, soul and copious amounts of tears as I described my symptoms. "Please tell me I'm not crazy," I sobbed.

After observing the wailing wreck in front of him, he spoke a few words which completely changed everything. "You are not crazy, and yes I think you have Chronic Fatigue Syndrome." The relief I felt at that moment was immense. A massive weight dropped away from my shoulders with this reassurance that I wasn't actually losing my mind. This man believed me and believed my symptoms and could help me. No longer did I have to fight, battle, and scream for help. The only thing stopping me leaping onto him and hugging him was the fact that I was exhausted, looked like a wreck and was covered with snot.

Following his diagnosis, I sat boldly upright listening intently, hanging on to his every word. He told me that if I looked after myself, and rehabilitated myself by alternating gentle activities with rest periods, then I probably wouldn't end up in a wheelchair. I returned home and began to follow his advice. I also began to research Chronic Fatigue Syndrome, to find out what else could be done. Now that I had a diagnosis, I could begin to help myself, and aid my recovery. Reading that acupuncture could be beneficial, I booked in for my first session at our local community hospital. I arrived with my two-year-old son, and the therapist, after a little investigation, asked me to lie on my side on the couch and just relax. My son took advantage of the warm blanket underneath, snuggled his tiny body into mine, and slept. When questioned, I talked about my health in depth and discussed the panic attacks. I told her that it just felt like I'd forgotten how to breathe correctly and that I didn't know what a normal breathing pattern was anymore. Her kindness and compassion helped immensely. After lying on the couch for just ten minutes, I experienced an epiphany. For the first time in a very long time I was relaxed. It dawned on me that I'd literally forgotten how to relax. Has there ever been a time in your life when you have been so focused on being a 'human doing' that you have forgotten how to just be a 'human being'? Has there been a time when you have convinced yourself that you were an indestructible machine? I'd been so busy bouncing off the walls teaching fitness classes and being a busy mum and wife I'd forgotten how to take care of me. Soon after, the acupuncturist inserted the needles. Following the treatment I felt as though I'd slept for a week, refreshed and relaxed.

CHANGING ROOM TIP
The Most Important Person Is You

How well do you maintain yourself and your body? I previously thought that I needed to put everyone else and their needs first. Being a mother, my children always were and still are everything to me, and I am and will always be driven to do my absolute best to ensure that they feel loved and cared for. It's an innate response that will always be there and it's very, very important. Feeling so strongly about this, I thought that as long as everyone else around me was looked after, I would be fine. But this approach obviously didn't work because eventually I broke.

A lovely therapist once told me, "The most important person in your life is you." It took me a while to make sense of this, but it's now something I live my life by, and you should too. If you are familiar with flying, you will be aware of the safety briefing given on every flight before take-off. You hear the words, "In the unlikely event of oxygen levels dropping in the cabin, the oxygen masks will automatically drop. Parents, please ensure that you put on your own masks first, before placing them on your children." As a parent, those words are hard to deal with. How could it possibly be right to put yourself before your children? What feels difficult to do is what you must do. Unless you are looking after yourself, you are not in good health to look after others.

If you look after yourself, and ensure that you get to relax, go out with friends, laugh, smile, and fulfil your needs, then you will be in a much better place to support and love those around you. If you are a parent reading this, your children need to be taught how to be happy and healthy, so lead by example. The biggest gift you can ever give your children is to teach them how to 'live'. Our bodies and minds are intricate systems which need regular care and maintenance, particularly rest and relaxation. You can choose to live your life with your foot flat down on the accelerator, hurtling along at an immense speed, doing your utmost to be perfect and get everything done. This though, is totally unsustainable and it won't be long before you come to a grinding halt, broken and too exhausted to move.

CHANGING ROOM TIP

Recognise Your Reds

My advice is to drive fast when you have to, but notice the traffic lights. Sometimes you need to stop completely, other times you need to slow down, and other times you need to keep going. Ensure that you have varied 'red, amber and green' days in every week. Give yourself permission to have at least one red day every week, or one red hour every day.

What is your red?

Think about what your 'red' could be right now. Is it a gentle stroll in the park? Lunch with friends? A massage? Yoga or meditation?

Make a list of all of your possible 'reds' and begin to incorporate these into your daily life. Don't just think about them, but commit to them by putting them on your calendar or in your diary. Re-educate yourself with red! Start today!

My Reds:

1.

2.

3.

4.

5.

6.

7.

8.

9.

10.

My investigations into healing led me towards holistic massage and reflexology, which quickly became 'reds' for me. Having these treatments on a regular basis, I was astounded at the depth of relaxation I achieved. My panic attacks began to subside dramatically, and I began to feel calmer and more energised. Following the advice of the specialist, my activity periods became longer as I recovered. My rest periods became shorter and very slowly, I had to give my poor husband a break and start doing housework again. (Damn it.) Very gradually, I began to re-dress, reaching out and grabbing all that I wore before and had discovered following my hair loss. Still slightly ruffled, I smoothed myself down after this unexpected blip and went back to my 'normal' life, a little older and wiser. My new short blonde maximum-volume wig symbolised a fresh start. Along with my new knowledge, I had discovered a newfound respect for my body. Eventually, I increased my fitness teaching hours again, but regularly gave my body the chance to experience rest and relaxation.

Having Chronic Fatigue Syndrome taught me a lot about myself. It taught me that I didn't relax often enough. It also taught me that holistic therapies and therapies incorporating the power of touch are great healers. Inspired by these medicines, my interest in this field was ignited. To keep the flame alive, and following my intuition, I decided to train as both a holistic massage therapist and reflexologist. The courses and the knowledge lit me up inside. I discovered that giving treatments produced wonderful health-giving benefits both for me and for the people that I practised on. I began to thrive on inducing relaxing, healing states within others. Learning more about the body excited me, and linked with all the anatomy and physiology that I had previously studied as a fitness instructor. As a result, my knowledge regarding the body, health and well-being became far more deeply integrated.

Wanting others to experience the power of deep relaxation, I set up my own part-time business offering both holistic massage and reflexology. During this time, I also continued to teach fitness classes. My life was healthy and balanced, and I found that being a therapist gave me a strong sense of peace. Through this, I began to experience deep feelings of interconnectedness with people and with the world. People would come not only for a treatment, but to talk. My clients would often pour out their hearts, and I would listen and empathise. During treatments, I would imagine connecting with my clients, sending them healing and white light from my heart. I truly believed that they felt my intentions, and that my intentions made a difference. Whilst giving a reflexology treatment one morning, massaging the area on the foot that corresponded with the heart, I had yet another epiphany. Was it possible that I had reached an advanced stage of silver-lining spotting? Chronic Fatigue had unveiled a new gift: the gift to help others take time out both physically and emotionally.

*I AM THE MOST IMPORTANT
PERSON IN MY LIFE*

I WILL REST

I WILL PLAY

I WILL LOVE

I WILL LAUGH

I WILL MOVE

I WILL NOURISH

I WILL NURTURE

I WILL GROW

I WILL LEARN

*I WILL FILL MYSELF WITH
HAPPINESS*

*AND LET IT SPILL OUT ONTO
OTHERS.*

ADDING MORE LAYERS

Enjoying my new gift and continuing to feel happy, I sat at home one morning having a 'red moment' with a coffee. Browsing through a magazine, I noticed an advert promoting a life-coaching course. My heart communicated with me by sending bubbles once again through my veins, a surge of undeniable excitement. Knowing that acting upon that urge had brought me benefits in the past, I did a little investigation. Within minutes I found myself picking up the phone and booking a place. Oblivious to what life coaching really involved, I was driven by a burning desire to find out. It wasn't a want, it was a necessity. I'd loved motivating people physically over the years, and it left me wondering how amazing it would be to help them psychologically too.

One month later, I found myself on the course, in a room full of people all with the same curiosity. It quickly became evident that there were a lot of people in the room who had been through adversity at some point in their lives. Many had been naked, had rebuilt their lives, and were reborn with a desire to help others. It was lovely to be in the company of so many like-minded 'nudie graduates'. For the first time in my life, I experienced an overwhelming sense of belonging. Was it possible that I had found my tribe?

After just a few short days, it was if I'd stepped into an unknown but very, very exciting world. Was it really true we were born with infinite potential? Could it be true that there was a world without limits, in which anything was possible?

Learning to coach and ask very powerful questions which drew out powerful and revealing answers in my colleagues, I began to see evidence of this.

It was my first encounter with the power of belief, and the first time that I ever heard these words:

"What you believe about yourself may not be true."

This comment totally floored me and challenged what I thought was my reality. You may be sensing the same confusion right now!

These words led me to reflect on my own personal experiences. What had I believed throughout my challenges? It suddenly dawned on me that in my early nakedness having lost my hair, I had initially formulated the idea or 'belief' that I was ugly, that no one would like me and that I had no purpose. I had in the past created this belief, or 'pain-inducing story', to help me make sense of my situation. What had created the belief that I was ugly or a misfit without hair? Probably years of reading magazines with airbrushed supermodels on the front covers, surrounded by words such as 'body beautiful' and 'glossy locks' amongst other things. My life changed spectacularly when I consciously changed this belief. I decided to believe instead that 'I may be without hair but it has happened for a positive reason.' Wow. I've lived what I'm teaching.

CHANGING ROOM TIP

Bust Your Beliefs
(separate fact from fiction)

What do you believe about you?

Beliefs can empower or restrict us. Standing lost and vulnerable, we often feel restricted by our beliefs about what we think there is, or what we think is possible.

Many of our beliefs are formed in our childhood, as we learn, grow and make sense of the world around us. Our beliefs began as ideas, or 'tiny seeds' in the garden of our unconscious minds. These seeds may have been planted by parents, by friends, or by people expressing their authority. We want to make sense of the world that we live in, so our minds begin to look for evidence to prove that these ideas are true.

We look for evidence that 'we are not clever enough', or 'not good enough', and what we look for we find. Every tiny piece of evidence becomes a root that sustains our seeds; well fed and watered they then grow into limiting beliefs which not only dramatically influence our behaviour, but our life. Our beliefs become our reality. We end up living in a smaller world, boxed in by our beliefs. Happiness cannot be found in a smaller world. It waits patiently for you to notice its presence on the outside.

The good news is that if your beliefs are preventing you from becoming who you want to be, they can be changed. You may feel tied down by heavy chains, but look down. The truth is, you hold onto them. And if YOU are holding onto them, then YOU can let go!

> *"We are not here to make believe, we are here to believe we can make it."*
>
> Guru Singh

Lost in adversity, and in our confusion, our negative beliefs may seem overwhelming. On reflection we can see that we are holding onto the heavy chains very tightly indeed, in an attempt to find some control, or make sense of our reality. What may help us make sense of it all temporarily will cause long-term pain. Holding onto heavy chains confines us and becomes tiring. Freedom comes when we choose to let go. Without chains we rise.

Sophie's Story

A 40-year-old lady booked in for one of my four-hour Breakthrough Sessions. She was obviously desperate for help and seeking a breakthrough. As we worked together, it became evident that she felt lost, numb, and dead inside. We discussed her life in great detail, and she told me that she had a great husband and three lovely children, but hated her job and felt unfulfilled. Through her tears, she revealed that she had been in the same job since she was 16 years old. For 24 years she had been working in a windowless office filing and carrying out very basic secretarial duties. Sensing that this was feeding her negative emotion, I asked if she had ever contemplated looking for another job or re-training in another field.

"I'm just not clever enough," she replied, looking down, tears spilling to the floor.

Noticing the very prominent limiting belief, I questioned as to how she knew this was true. She told me that it had been the story of her life, that she had never been that clever. Exploring further I asked her how she knew she wasn't clever. It was something that people had always told her, she said. I continued to question her: "Who specifically has told you this?" I watched as her eyes searched her head for the answers, confusion evident upon her face. Confusion turned into recognition as she found her answer. "My mother," she replied.

I questioned her as to when her mother had last told her that she wasn't clever. Confusion yet again before she delivered her answer.

"I remember, I remember... It was our seventh birthday party [referring to herself and her twin sister]. My mother brought one of her friends over and introduced us. She said, "This is Sophie the sporty one, and this is Veronica the mathematician."

"See, even at a very young age she branded me un-academic." Satisfied with her answer, she sat back and sniffed. I asked her what other evidence she had to prove this, and after giving it much thought, these were some of her answers:

1. *Failing to be picked for the school quiz team in primary school*
2. *Failing some tests at the end of primary school*
3. *Her mother saying to her at the age of sixteen, "I've found you a job with a family friend, you won't find anything better."*

Sophie had found her seed (the beginnings of her negative belief) at the age of seven, and having fed and watered it well over the years, she totally believed that she could be or have no more. It was 100% her reality.

Then came the killer question. "Sophie, how do you know that at seven years old, your mother wasn't simply trying to help you, as twins, find separate identities?"

Confusion.

"How do you know it wasn't just a passing comment that meant very little at all?"

Further confusion.

"What if your sister wasn't very good at sport?"

"She wasn't," she replied. Again her eyes searched for answers, then Sophie got what she needed. Speechless, she looked at me directly and I asked her if it was possible that she had lived the last 24 years believing she wasn't clever enough, based on one comment made by her mother all those years

ago. "That appears to be true," she whispered trying to make sense of her new learning, as she sat in stunned silence. We explored evidence to suggest that she was clever, and she was astounded at how much we discovered. Just a few moments later, Sophie sat upright, receptive and hanging onto my every word about her future. Sophie had been confined by her thoughts just as a bird is confined in a cage, and she had just realised that the cage door had always been open.

Sophie did fly, and to great new heights, unleashing her potential along the way, and she continues to be happy to this day.

All she did was change one belief.

Think about your life right now. What beliefs are you holding onto that place restrictions on what you could do, or who you could be? If you are not living the life that you want and find it difficult to move forwards, an underlying limiting belief could very well be the cause. And remember, what you believe about yourself may not be true.

If what you believe about yourself isn't true, then surely it can be compared to living a lie? Wouldn't it be better to be honest and live your truth? It's not as difficult as you may believe! You weren't born with limiting beliefs, and probably lived a good few years without them before they developed. No one is ever born with limiting beliefs. All you need to do is go back to who you really are. It's about separating the fact from the fiction and returning to who you were always meant to be.

Here's a simple process that will help you eradicate and change your limiting beliefs. It's time to separate your fact from fiction, truth from lies. Put pen to paper now, and answer these questions as honestly as possible:

What are you not getting in your life that you would like?

What do you say to yourself that stops you from getting this?

Based on that information, what is your limiting belief?

Where did this belief come from?

What evidence have you got to support this belief?

What evidence have you got to suggest that this belief is untrue?

Who would you be without this belief?

What would be a more empowering belief to have?

Who would you be with this new belief?

Can you see a reason to try out this new belief?

Your challenge now is to try out this new belief. Imagine suspending your old belief in mid air temporarily (you can always take it back should you choose). Imagine that your new belief is a whole new outfit, and you get to wear it for a day. If you enjoy the results that you get, then it's highly likely that you will choose to wear it for longer periods. The more you wear it, the more natural it will become.

Believe in you, your potential and your capabilities. You are far too amazing and beautiful to be tainted by untruths.

Following the completion of the life-coaching course, I sat with my head against the window on the train journey home and cried. Tears of happiness poured down my face. For the first time ever, every single part of my personal journey suddenly made sense. I decided that I was meant to lose my hair, I was meant to have Chronic Fatigue Syndrome. I had to get naked, not just once, but twice to learn enough. My calling and purpose was crystal clear: I was put on this planet to help others get through their struggles, find happiness through adversity and live their dreams. I needed to help people climb out of their darkness and towards their light, and to enable them to re-connect with their soul and strength. My purpose was to seek out the naked people, and help them re-dress with happiness. A huge grin spread across my face, with a knowing; a knowing that for the first time in my life I was conscious of and experiencing self love. And I knew that I'd found my way home to my heart. The warmth inside me just had to spill out onto others, because right now, I was on fire.

CHANGING ROOM TIP

Feed Your Soul

You can spend a lifetime trying to make sense of your head, or you can simply follow your heart.

We are born with hungry souls, seeking nourishment to thrive, grow and be happy. As young children we feed our souls all that they need by doing what we love. As time passes, we stop doing what we love as we are influenced by other people's expectations and opinions. We start to starve our souls to feed others. A typical example of this is the teenager who at 16 years old feels pressured to choose the 'right' career. The teen may be an exceptional dancer, singer or artist but is persuaded by others to get a 'proper', 'sensible', traditional job. The dancer starves his soul as his sits in an office in front of a computer all day. The singer becomes an accountant and ignores the screams from within. The artist locks away her paints and canvas and dreams of what could have been. Starved souls beg for change but their cries are lost in the chaos of busy living.

What happens if you constantly feed your body the wrong food? A lifetime of junk food, alcohol and smoking will damage your body significantly. The likelihood of you getting sick would be very high. Your soul is no different, it needs to be fed appropriately to avoid the mind becoming ill, symptoms often being anxiety and depression.

What food are you serving to your soul every day?

In stillness and solitude, it's not uncommon for souls to make their feelings known through words. Have you ever said or thought: "I never thought I'd end up in a job like this," or "I didn't ever dream of doing what I'm doing now."? You didn't dream of it because you weren't meant to be doing it. Fact.

Having lost touch with their souls (often influenced by others), I often hear my clients say, "I don't know what I want to do, how can I possibly move forwards?" The truth is, it doesn't really matter what you do as long as you do something, and do something that makes you smile. It's that simple.

What difference would it make to your life if you stepped out of your comfort zone and into something new? Right now think about three things that would excite you. Choose the one which excites you the most. (A great tip: If you can't choose between two of them, toss a coin, let it land on the floor and step on it before you look at it. Ask yourself, "Which one did I WANT it to land on?" Your heart will answer.)

CHANGING ROOM TIP

What You Choose Does Not Have To Be Where You End Up

The pressure of finding the 'right thing' to move forwards can sometimes be overwhelming and prevent us from progressing at all. But what if there were no right thing? If you follow your heart it cannot be the wrong thing, it's not possible. If you feel compelled to try or to learn something new right now in your life, then go and do it. It may not be where you eventually end up, but it will contribute greatly to your learning and open up possibilities that didn't previously exist.

I have had three very different careers, but the knowledge gained in all of them gives me more knowledge than many with regards to health, fitness and wellbeing. Together they are a very powerful force and their combined knowledge drives me forwards intensely in every aspect of my career today.

Everything that you do or learn lays down roots for your future. The more roots you have, the better your fruit will taste! If you have no idea at all what to do, then follow my next changing room tip:

CHANGING ROOM TIP

Make An Appointment With Yourself

My top tip is to book an appointment with 'you' for half a day. Put it in your diary, or on your calendar. Block the time out and guard it with your life. Stand sentry to your soul. Take yourself to a quiet café, or a beautiful place in nature, and sit and write down every idea you have. Draw or write every possibility that springs to mind. Allow your heart to power your pen. When you have a list, grade each idea from 1 to 10, 1 being 'don't really want to do it' to 10, 'I'd love to do it'. Pick one or two of your ideas with the highest numbers and ask yourself these questions:

"What do I need to do to make this happen?"

"When can I start to make this happen?"

Then make it happen.

A thought for you:

There were ten parrots sat on a perch. Three decided to fly away. How many remained? You may be thinking seven. The answer is ten because they only decided, they didn't follow through. Don't be the parrot left on the perch. Take action today.

FOOD FOR THE BODY IS NOT ENOUGH. THERE MUST BE FOOD FOR THE SOUL.

Dorothy Day

THE THIRD GIFT

Returning home as a life coach, feeling on top of the world, my knowledge was bursting out. My family and friends found themselves unknowingly led into coaching conversations as I tried out my new techniques. I practised relentlessly, trying to coach everyone that I came into contact with. I tried it at the supermarket check-out, at the bus stop, in my fitness classes and with my poor husband continually. Quickly realising that not everyone wants to change, I had to find another way. My only option was to immediately set up in business as a coach. It wasn't just a want, it was a necessity. My internal flames were roaring so fiercely I was in danger of spontaneous human combustion. I had to find a way to conduct the heat.

Recognising that I couldn't run three businesses effectively, and having learnt from previous experiences, I decided to step back from my work as a holistic therapist whilst I launched my coaching career. I proudly painted an office at the back of my husband's business premises from which to work: The Changing Room. I wrote an article for the local newspaper declaring my intention and took business cards to everyone that I knew. My newfound career was dropped into as many conversations as possible, and people became curious. Anyone that showed interest and stood still for more than ten seconds got to know what I could do for them. I was a life coach. I could change lives. The strong belief that the skills that I had learnt and developed could help many fuelled my drive to succeed.

Office decorated, I sat in my new brown leather-look chair and waited for my newly installed telephone to ring. A few days later it did, and people began to come. Lives began to change and I felt as if I had truly found my purpose in life. A deep spiritual awakening that was very new to me was taking place. It felt both humbling and exceptionally fulfilling. The first ever client that I worked with gave me two tiny pink candles in a beautiful little organza bag to say thank you at our last session. I still treasure these candles today.

I began to work with many clients with varying issues, but found that I was struggling to help those holding onto problems from their past. I began to investigate the field of Neuro Linguistic Programming (NLP), as this had been recommended as further study. I had no idea what NLP was, but I was captivated by one description that called it 'The Art Of Excellence'. As I researched I discovered that it encompassed neurology, language and mind programming. The more I discovered, the more I felt compelled to pursue this knowledge. My husband Paul, knowing me well, began noticing evidence of champagne in my veins yet again. Having seen me flit from career to career he became increasingly and thoroughly exasperated. "Not another course! When are you going to stop doing courses?" he exclaimed whilst I discussed with him my new and exciting interest. At that time I really didn't know the answer. What I did know, though, was that following my heart was continually increasing my happiness. It also occurred to me that my heart had never, ever got it wrong.

A short time later, on a four-day NLP diploma course, yet another world opened up. I explored my own life with the help of others. Reflecting back upon my past I gained many new and liberating insights and felt empowered. For the very first time, I glimpsed the true power of communication, personal development and psychology.

Having embraced her nakedness, the once bald, weak woman stood strong; so strong that nothing could ever take her away from herself again...

Isn't it amazing that when you think you are floating in euphoria, on top of the world, the wind can suddenly change yet again? Because that's what happened, in the form of pain in my left hip.

Still teaching fitness, I had diverged into the field of combat-style fitness which involved various combinations of non-contact kicks and punches. I first noticed the pain during and after these classes and it quickly progressed into pain in the night. Shooting, excruciating pains often woke me from my sleep; it felt as if someone was driving a very large needle down the front of my thigh. Several diagnoses of hip strain and visits to the physiotherapist didn't help. The pain just continued to get worse and I found myself limping often, hardly able to walk in a straight line. After one particular class the pain was so intense I could barely get back to my car. I called my husband to tell him that in desperation, I was driving myself to hospital. I limped into accident and emergency, half expecting to be sent away as a time waster. Fortunately, it was a quiet evening and they were happy to examine me, sensing my frustration. The doctor sent me for an X-ray, and I sat in the hospital cubicle to await the results. Anticipating that the results would come back normal, I sat back and waited. At least I would be reassured and be able to stop worrying. I simply needed to hear that there was nothing majorly wrong so that I could continue with the life that I loved so much.

Forty-five minutes later, I didn't get what I needed. The doctor returned with a solemn look on his face. He sat on a stool opposite me and then told me that at the age of 35, I had hip dysplasia. He explained that my hip socket wasn't quite the right shape, and the pain that I had been experiencing was probably due to the instability of the joint. He then added that I would need a major operation to correct it.

My face draining of all colour, I sat and tried to delete what I had just heard. Delete. Delete. Delete. No luck, because his words wouldn't disappear, I just heard them over and over again. I sat frozen to my seat and noticed that my hands were shaking. I looked at the doctor in desperation. Tears spilled from my eyes, as I tried to make sense of what he was saying. "I can't have an operation, I'm a fitness instructor, it's my job, my life," I whispered in disbelief. "Fitness is how I got my life back." He looked at me with pity and really didn't know what to say.

Staggering back to the car park, my body fell into my vehicle in shock, every part of me trembling. I called my husband, barely able to breathe or talk, with tears pouring down my face. My whole world and everything in it was about to disappear once more, together with my identity. I sobbed as I told him the news. He attempted to calm me but right there and then, losing my career as a fitness instructor, all I had ever known for many years, filled me with fear and dread. What the hell had I done to deserve this? Hadn't I already been through enough? Why me? Why is my fitness career, what I love to do, constantly being torn away? I screamed, I cried, drove halfway home and pulled over into a lay-by. I screamed again, hitting the steering wheel repeatedly, hoping that it was all a bad dream and that I would wake up. Unfortunately I wasn't sleeping.

Days of shock, feelings of devastation and sorrow followed as I allowed myself some time to deal with the impact. Yes, I moved into 'the home of misery' to wail and feel self-pity for a few days, but it slowly dawned on me that, based on past experiences, I had tools to get me through. Feeling emotionally bruised and sore I got back up and started moving.

I was going to fight another round. I would not give up and I would certainly not be beaten. "You've been through so much already, you've lost all your hair, you've been wearing a wig for years, you've gone through Chronic Fatigue and panic attacks," I told myself. "You can get through this."

CHANGING ROOM TIP
Go One More Round

Stuff happens. Sometimes we get knocked down in life, find our way back up, and then get knocked down again. Life isn't always straightforward, plans are turned upside down overnight, leaving us feeling exhausted and in despair. Straightforward, however, can be boring. Straightforward is predictable, safe, certain, and, to be honest, not that exciting.

I'm not suggesting that severe challenge or adversity is exciting, because sometimes it's pretty damned hard. But if we find the strength to get back up and fight one more round, then we learn and we get stronger. Stronger with knowledge we have the ability to lead more fulfilling lives. But we need to get up and fight one more round. If we don't get up, we know with absolute certainty that we will remain at rock bottom.

> *By getting up, you give yourself the chance and permission to pursue happiness. Fighting one more round may well bring you victory.*

Deciding that I wanted to go one more round, it was time to bring out the toolbox. Focusing on learnings from my past experiences, I was determined to use these to get through come hell or high water. I knew that I needed to think about this challenge in a different way. Finding spiritual solitude on an early morning visit to the beach, I asked myself this question: "What's the best thing about this happening to you?" I sat in stillness, watching the waves, and waited for the answers to roll in. They arrived as they always do, in a set:

1. I will have more time to study more about coaching
2. I will have more time to study NLP
3. I won't have to work evenings teaching fitness classes (a welcome break)
4. I can still life coach sitting in a wheelchair or on crutches

I returned home more than satisfied with the revelations, spirit fed and watered.

Bringing back the old and very well-installed acceptance strategy, combined with viewing the situation from a different perspective, gave me relief from my emotional pain and anger. It virtually disappeared overnight. Incredibly, I found myself becoming grateful for my most recent challenge. (I even wrote it in my gratitude book.) Negative feelings dissipated, replaced with feelings of excitement and new growth. The medical diagnosis had initially floored me, but I had risen and was prepared to rise further to take on the challenge. I would not be beaten. I knew who I was now.

A few weeks later I found myself sitting in front of a surgeon who spoke of the operation that I would be having, a Periacetabular Osteotomy. This apparently involved breaking my hip socket into three pieces to reform it into a better shape. The broken bones would then be held together with screws. The surgeon informed me that my recovery and rehabilitation would be a long process, and that patience would need to be my strongest virtue. My intention was to have it done as soon as possible so that I could return to my life sooner rather than later; but it didn't quite go to plan. The operation was cancelled twice. The operation that I was having was extremely rare; apparently the tools necessary to chop me up were being borrowed from elsewhere and hadn't yet arrived at the hospital.

Awaiting the operation my hip deteriorated by the day and the pain increased. A cocktail of strong painkillers were needed to help me sleep at night, but left me feeling 'drugged' every morning when I awoke: sleepy, sick, and dizzy. Frustrated and desperate I felt the negative thoughts making their presence known. Raising the bar yet again I decided to book onto a higher level of NLP training to fill my mind with more positive things. This had worked in the past. Still waiting for a date for this seemingly impossible operation, I started the course thirsty for new knowledge. Knowing that finishing this course would give me a huge new set of skills, I totally immersed myself in my studies. Reading, researching, writing, and practising became my daily routine. My bookshelf at home began to bend with new literature. Any book that I could find to teach me more found its way to my letterbox, and my favourite place on earth became the psychology and self-help sections at Waterstones. I became fascinated and obsessed by the stories of others who had faced adversity, and the strategies that they had used to overcome their challenges. Reading real-life stories, I realised that many of the people had used similar strategies to emerge from adversity as I had. It turned out that the world had always been, and still was, full of people wandering around naked. I just hadn't seen it before. My sense of belonging grew stronger as did my skill set as a coach.

I continued to attend the course, and not only grew my knowledge but made some amazing new friends with exceptional spirit levels. My tribe was growing. There's no quicker way to connect with another soul than working through the strategies and techniques of Neuro Linguistic Programming. Exposing vulnerabilities to a total stranger soon makes them a trusted friend. It was one of these trusted friends that one day guided me through an exceptionally powerful process that allowed me to truly step into my soul and my inner wisdom. That day I gave my soul the freedom to speak loud and clear, and hear the words that would empower me for many years to come. I'd like to guide you through the following process right now, to enable you to tap into your true potential and being. Let your soul be the guide. Find a place of calm and peace (your soul will speak loudly in silence) and answer the following questions. Give yourself as much time as you need, and ensure that you write the answers down. You will need to refer to them afterwards.

CHANGING ROOM TIP

Allow The Soul To Speak

Imagine that you are 'you from the future' and have had the opportunity to float back in time to see the 'you of today' stood or sat right in front of you. What would your words of advice be to the current you?

Imagine that you are a 'friend from the future'. Someone who cares about you very much and has had the ability to float back in time and speak to the 'you of today'. What advice would you give?

Imagine that you are someone very important to you in your life, someone you care about very much. Imagine standing in their shoes, seeing what they see, hearing what they hear and feeling what they feel. As this person, what advice would you give to the 'you of today'?

Bring someone from your past to mind, someone who was very important to you who is not in your life any more. Maybe a friend, teacher, relation? Imagine that you are this person, giving the 'you of today' some words of advice. What do you want to say?

Imagine that you are a small child, unrelated to the 'this being' of today. Small children have the ability see to a situation as uncomplicated, and therefore sometimes give the best, simplest advice!

As a small child, what do you want to say to the 'you of today'?

Imagine now that you are a presence from your past. A wise, caring presence that has watched over your being for many, many years. As this presence you have witnessed everything that this 'being' has been through and you give the best advice from your heart. What do you want to say?

Imagine now that you are a very wise and spiritual presence, living in the moment. The only knowledge that you have regarding this 'being' is current. Having the ability to help others find their strength and tune into their wisdom, deliver the best advice possible.

Bring to mind right now someone you know who has pulled through adversity. It could be a friend or somebody famous, or even a character in a film. Imagine that you are this person, and that you want to give the 'you of today' some advice.
What would you say?

Now that you have completed the exercise, take a deep breath before reading back the answers to yourself, one by one. Read them out loud. For extra power, record your voice (perhaps on your mobile phone) and play it back. Then play it back again.

Notice the feelings that arise as you hear your words. And notice that though you were looking at your situation from a range of very different perspectives, those very powerful words came from your lips, and from your mind. The truth is, you have you an exceptional therapist on call 24/7 in the form of your soul, which patiently waits in every second of every hour of every day for your permission to speak.

There is never a better time than now to connect with your truth. Standing naked means that the words have fewer layers to get through. They can be easily heard, as struggling whispers are replaced with strong powerful directions, guidance loud and clear. There is never a better time than now. Life is short. And we only get one chance.

I AM YOUR SOUL

I am your soul. I have all of the answers that you need. You listened to me as a young child, but then silenced me as you grew. You became what you thought you should be, instead of what you could be. I know that you have felt my presence over the years, as I've whispered from within. But you were too busy to listen. I missed you.

I love that you are naked. I love that you cannot find answers elsewhere. I love that the only answers you have are my answers. I love that you have chosen to listen to me and trust my truth and wisdom. I love working with you. I love you. Long may we be together as one.

INTERNAL ADJUSTMENTS

A few weeks later a third crisp white envelope with the hospital stamp marked 'Private and Confidential' made its way to my letterbox. The tools must have arrived. My operation appeared to be scheduled in three weeks' time, bang in the middle of my NLP Practitioner training. After another "Why does everything good I do get taken away?" thought, I contacted Nick Evans, the trainer, and discussed my options. It became clear that my only available option was to wait a whole year to catch up on the next course. "Accept it. Get over it. Move on. Move it to the back of your mind." I told myself, and that's what I tried to do, but the call of passion and purpose just kept coming back. My desires were trying strongly to make themselves known. The voice within seemed to rise in volume by the day. The thoughts simply wouldn't go away. Why wasn't acceptance working this time?

Three weeks later I wasn't very happy and neither was my skin. I was opened up and what can only be described as internally butchered. Slowly waking after the operation I felt incredibly sick and looked as if I'd been locked in a room with a hungry werewolf. When I discovered the catheter I felt even sicker: I'd forgotten I'd have the pleasure of a catheter. I spent the next two days incoherent and in tremendous pain. A nurse, wanting to help, asked me if I wanted to try 'Tramadol' for a change; Tramadol sounded quite a cool drug with a hip name so I thought I'd give it a go. Unfortunately my body decided that it wasn't quite so hip but rather vomit inducing. It took me on a spaced-out mind trip to the bottoms of many hospital cardboard bowls. It was grim. I recall my concerned parents coming to visit me. I sat in bed, sweat pouring down my face in rivulets. Trying to make sense of their words seemed impossible in my drugged state. The humming of the fan strategically placed to cool me gave me a focus. It was the only thing that I knew was absolutely real.

The following day I decided that physical pain was preferable to 'tripping out' and going to cardboard bowl land, so I chose to reduce my medication. The pain was still intense but at least I knew where I was, and who I was.

The heat of the hospital resulted in my head feeling incredibly itchy under my wig, and for the first time in fourteen years, I nervously contemplated going without. Looking at the rest of my body, I guessed it couldn't really get any worse and to be honest I was probably past caring. I lay in the bed figuring out how to take it off without shocking the other patients. Was it okay to just suddenly remove my hair? Where do I put it when I take it off? Do I leave it on the cabinet beside me, or shut it in the cupboard to shock a nurse? Where do wigs live? Summoning up all my strength, I simply pulled it off and chucked it in the bedside cabinet. I felt very conspicuous but liberated. My head felt cool and free. What were the other patients thinking? Quickly realising that all of the other patients on the ward were probably as doped up as I'd been, I concluded that the last thing on their mind was my weird head. I was a little self-conscious when people came to visit, as most had never seen me without my wig. By this time however, I had just been through so much emotional and physical pain that it just didn't seem to matter. I'm me. Take it or leave it.

The following day was 'dressing change day' and I wasn't prepared for the sight of the twenty large chunky staples that held my nine-inch wound together. If I hadn't been lying down I would have fainted. Had I been asked beforehand, I would have requested two hundred stitches rather than staples; there is something very macabre about being held together with metal. As they changed the bloody dressing, I distracted myself by imagining walking through airport security as I was. Can you even imagine how much I would beep?! My gaze returned to my wound and I considered taking a photo of it. I wondered if I could get a role in a horror movie as a kidnapped and tortured victim. Realising that most murderers don't generally insert catheters into their victims, I decided that maybe I wouldn't get the part, so decided to stay put and recover. Whilst lying in bed I examined the photo of my post-op X-ray. I could see various screws but also a strange long twisted-looking object. Confused, I questioned the doctor as to its identity. It turned out the drill bit broke off during the procedure and they couldn't get it out. (It stills sits inside me today.)

A day later was 'catheter removal day' and my bladder was back to *au naturel*. I was now allowed to empty in a bedpan; not the most pleasurable experience. For those of you that know me, bladder strength has never been my forte, and I know that I must have tested the patience of the nurse. I requested bedpans every hour. On one particular day, I was very lucky (or the nurses were sick to death of running around after me) because I was that evening allowed to sit in a chair next to my bed and use a commode. It was a very strange feeling being vertical after being horizontal for so many days. My muscles had slightly atrophied so were weak and I felt dizzy. My bladder was delighted however and I'm sure I heard it scream, "Yay, gravity!"

The following morning I was introduced to my new aid: a Zimmer frame. Not being allowed to bear weight at all on the operated side, I had to learn to slowly hobble along using just my right leg, pushing the frame forwards to gain ground. The thought of getting it wrong and falling onto my side and onto twenty staples kept appearing in my mind. This didn't help my confidence so I quickly chose to eradicate it and just focus on getting where I needed to go. I eventually managed to hobble to the toilets all by myself, which was a huge relief: bladder freedom at last!

Two days later I was introduced to my crutches, my two new shiny friends who would remain by my side for weeks to come. The physiotherapist spent time with me, attempting to get me walking with them, but the fear of falling was so great that I just froze, time and time again. I felt so weak, and so very vulnerable. My body refused to move even an inch. Exasperated, she said that she would return the following morning. Frustrated with my inability, I tried alone to no avail. What was wrong with me? Picking up the crutches filled me with fear. The thought of falling and breaking more bones or my wound bursting open was unbearable. I cried and cried some more. The next morning the physiotherapist returned and I was still obviously incapable. Thoroughly annoyed with her seemingly obstinate patient she gave up again. "We will not let you go home to your family until you can do this," she said, before stomping away. The thought of an extended stay was dreadful. I was finding the noisy ward, sleepless nights and lack of privacy a huge challenge.

Feeling anger at the physiotherapist's reaction (pain) and fuelled with thoughts of my family (pleasure), I picked up the crutches. Summoning up every ounce of courage, I focused on a spot two metres away on the floor. All I needed to do was to get to that spot. The other patients watched with amusement. Powered by anger and the people that I loved I took a wobbly step. Again and again I took tiny steps with the crutches, past the two-metre mark and then the three-metre mark before ending up in the middle of the ward. Overcome with joy, I stood supported by my crutches and sobbed in front of everyone. Having witnessed my previous struggles, the other patients began to applaud my achievement, which made me cry even more. After thanking my supporters, I looked out of the ward and towards the nurses' desk. I was aware that most staff knew of my apparent inability to use the crutches, after hearing a conversation between them and the physiotherapist. "I'll show them," I thought. I faced the nurses' desk, took a deep breath and took my steps to freedom. My steps got stronger and faster, and approaching the desk with a huge smile, I yelled, "I can do it!" The nurses laughed, before becoming increasingly concerned as I raced towards the exit. They must have been really worried as one nurse ran along the corridor and blocked my path. "It's okay," I laughed, sensing her fear. Realising that I didn't mean to walk all the way home, she relaxed.

Once I started, I just couldn't stop. Up the corridor, down the corridor, over and over again. The staff found my newfound enthusiasm entertaining and they joined me in my celebration, smiling and laughing as they watched the baldish lady who couldn't walk yesterday bound along. Once I'd passed the desk eight times however, they became more concerned. They told me to take a break and rest. "I'm fine," I said with a beaming smile. "I feel fantastic!" And I really did.

CHANGING ROOM TIP

Use Your Pivot Point To Burn Bridges

Your mindset will either hinder you or help you. Never have I experienced the power of a shift in mindset as I did that day in the hospital. My negative thoughts had literally paralysed me with fear: as much as I tried to move, I couldn't. (Have you ever wanted to move forwards so badly, but experienced the same paralysis?) The thoughts physically affected my body. The danger thoughts in my mind were protecting me, but also confining me. I was totally unaware that I was feeding my fear. The endless stories that I created in my mind, which involved falling, breaking bones, and wounds opening, created the paralysis.

In reality, I was held together with very strong screws and the experienced physiotherapist knew I was ready. In a heightened state of emotion (anger) and missing my family, I was able to turn my mind around and find the strength within. At that moment I burnt all bridges to any other possibility than success. And I achieved it.

Sometimes we get stuck in life. We don't think progress is possible. Imagine that you have a choice of two homes, only accessible by independent bridges. One is the home of happiness, the other the home of stagnation and pain. Having two bridges gives you one too many options. In deep emotional pain, you have the power to light the match and burn the bridge to stagnation and pain. You have the power to say, 'That's it. I've had enough. I'm not doing this anymore!' In the depths of sorrow and pain, there is a pivot point on which you can turn. Use it.

During pivotal moments, all will become clear. What you want and what you don't want will make themselves known, delivered in a message from your heart. Feel it and use it. Take that message, and focus on what you want to happen, and make it happen. Burn all bridges to any other possibility and bask in the warmth of the flames. It doesn't matter if you don't yet know how to get to the home of happiness. All that matters is that you have chosen the route, and made it the only possible way.

The following day, the physiotherapist returned, astounded at the empowered and overjoyed athlete that stood before her. After several attempts to practise climbing steps with my crutches on a wooden block in the middle of the ward, I was set free. I was wheeled out in a chair into daylight and fresh air and everything seemed so bright. Colours seemed vibrant and beautiful. I felt as if I'd been locked away forever. My poor husband was obviously excited to be taking me home to my children and was rushing around trying to get me to his van parked close by. It suddenly dawned on me that I was out in the real world with a huge wound, a very unstable hip and metal staples holding me together. Feeling unsafe in the outside world I burst into tears, creating quite a show of drama right outside the hospital entrance. After a prolonged emotional outburst, and having run out of tears, I eventually calmed down. I figured that I just needed to go slowly. Eventually I managed to get to the van, and with a little help I managed to get in and get home.

So much happier to be home, I was inundated with visits and help from friends, which helped a lot. Sleeping however was a challenge as I was only able to sleep on my back, and my poor husband could barely come near me. I tried sleeping with a 'V pillow', three pillows, five pillows, even in a chair but to no avail. The skin on my heels, bum and shoulders felt like it was burning as I spent so much time lying flat. Doctor's orders for six weeks. The pain in my hip was slowly replaced with pain all over my body.

Three days later whilst sitting at home, thoughts of the NLP course kept springing to mind, creating the familiar champagne-in-my-veins sensation. All that I could think about was the next module of the course, which would be taking place the coming weekend. Relentlessly it niggled away and gnawed at me. I dreamt about it at night and it was on my mind upon waking. How could I wait another year to really begin to help people? Three hundred and sixty five days was a very, very long time. Feeling like a volcano about to erupt, and trying to suppress my excitement, I very carefully and diplomatically put forwards my plan to my husband. I had to be careful because he was going to take some convincing.

I very directly informed my husband that although my body was limited, my mind was not. Therefore I could not see any reason why I couldn't take part in the next module of the course, due to start in just a couple of days. A look of horror came across his face as I asked him to drive me there; to a small wooden lodge, eighty miles away at the top of an icy hill. Knowing that I would be living there in the lodge alone for three days, and probably picturing me hurtling down a very large hill in a wheelchair, he refused point blank. Time to get out the extra ammunition. "If I have to be stuck sitting down, then I may as well be learning sitting down, and I can ask for help." I willed the tears to appear (and they did), and took a deep breath before delivering a grenade in the form of a killer line, "But you have worked so hard looking after me, I've kept you awake every night. You must be exhausted. You will get a break for three days." Sensing my steely determination and knowing that hell hath no fury like a suppressed Maria, he agreed. Plus the thought of a break from my demands was obviously tempting.

> *"The things that you are passionate about are not random, they are your calling."*
>
> Fabienne Fredrickson

CHANGING ROOM TIP
Connect With Your Purpose

Living your life with passion and purpose can be compared to having the elixir of life running through every vein, cell, and capillary.

If you have a desire to do something, do it. If you have a constant tap, tap, tap in your head, wake up and listen because it's your purpose crying out. It's shouting for your attention. You may choose to ignore and silence your purpose and opt for what you think is an easier life, walking a path laid by others. You can try as hard as you like to walk away from the truths within, and your calling. Just like a puppy dog at your heels, however, your calling will continue to make its presence known, trailing you like your shadow, nipping at your heels until you pay attention. The tap, tap in your head will become louder and the feeling of unease will become stronger. The short-term ease becomes long-term pain. Your calling will never disappear but becomes bigger and stronger as the years pass. If you don't live with purpose, you will most certainly live with regret. When faced with adversity, all the unimportant stuff fades away leaving only what makes our heart sing. You have never been closer to unveiling your purpose.

Ask yourself the questions below to help discover and connect with your purpose:

Have you ever felt a strong desire to do something?

What did you always dream of doing as a child?

What were you good at as a child?

What do you find yourself reading about on the internet in your spare time?

What do you do when you lose yourself in time? What are you doing when the hours pass quickly?

What are your natural skills and talents?

What would you regret NOT doing?

What lights you up inside and makes you feel plugged into life?

All of these questions will give clues to your calling. When you know what you love, you will know what to do. You just need to give yourself the chance. Don't wait another second, minute, or hour to connect with your purpose. Every moment living without it is a moment without happiness.

You can spend a lifetime trying to make sense of your head, or you can simply follow your heart.

FOLLOW YOUR PASSION, IT WILL LEAD TO YOUR PURPOSE.

Oprah Winfrey

PUSHING PAST LIMITS

Feeling proud of my determination, two days later I found myself back on the course, in a wheelchair and without my wig. Scary. No one on the course had seen me without it before, and I felt slightly worried about their initial reaction. Thankfully, everyone treated me as they had always done, which was positively reassuring. My heart had been right yet again. It wasn't the worst time to learn, but the best time. There were so many free hours to study, and ensure that my learnings were fully and deeply integrated. More books, relentless research, and more practice became my daily routine. My friends on the course helped me so much. They wheeled me up the icy slopes at the end of the day to my accommodation, and came to get me and wheel me back down again in the mornings to the training room. I will always be truly grateful for not only their kindness and patience, but for their humour which lifted me during challenging times. Trevor and Vanessa, it gives me great pleasure to thank you in writing. I learnt so much during those few days, not only about NLP but about those people who went out of their way to ensure that I remained safe and looked after. Acts of kindness were abundant during this time and I will always be eternally thankful.

CHANGING ROOM TIP

Show Your Strength And Ask For Help

Do you find it hard to ask for help? Does the fear of rejection stop you asking for assistance? Some believe that that asking for help is a sign of weakness. We've all experienced thoughts like these. In a wheelchair, with an insatiable appetite for new knowledge, I had no choice but to ask for help; it was the only way that I could achieve what I needed. I discovered that people loved to help me, showing extreme kindness, and I truly believe that our relationships were enhanced because of this.

During this time, I learnt that asking for help is a sign of strength. It's about knowing what you want, and making it happen. Learning to ask for help is about recognising that you don't have to go it alone. It's also about realising that people love to help, and want to be kind.

Who could you ask for help right now?

Who could you ask to support you in your journey?

What would this enable you to do?

How will this make you feel?

What difference could this make to your life, and your happiness?

CHANGING ROOM TIP
Improve Your Mind By Being Kind

(This changing room tip has a big space in this book, because it has a big space in not only my heart, but my life.)

Having been on the receiving end of much help, I began to truly understand the power of kindness and made it my mission to show more kindness myself. Acts of kindness have a huge hidden benefit; they will allow you to leave the selfish team, and allow you to grow self-esteem. Has that piqued your curiosity? Curiosity is the doorway to new knowledge, so read carefully and absorb, because these words are very, very important. In my early days of nakedness, I spent many hours, days, and weeks thinking about me, my situation, and my troubles. I became incredibly selfish (as many of us do) during this time, focusing on what was happening to me, with little thought to those who surrounded me. The more I thought about me, the worse and more bitter I felt, self-esteem dropping away by the day.

Through my own personal experiences, and those of my clients, I can honestly say that showing kindness to others is exceptionally powerful medicine for those experiencing adversity. Kindness redirects attention and focus. Imagine attention as a bright green ball. Feeling emotionally troubled, we commonly hold the ball tight to us, keeping all of our attention focused on how we personally feel. This state is highly unproductive as it restricts our thinking and keeps us 'boxed in' in our mind. We begin to believe that the emotions and feelings that we are experiencing are all that there is. We find it hard to see a way out.

Giving our attention to another person, or 'throwing the green ball' in our minds to them, takes our attention away from ourselves. A spectacular way to practise this is through delivering acts of kindness. When you focus on someone else, you will find it harder to stay focused on your problems. Your mind will be temporarily free from stress and worry as a result. The more you do this, the more free your mind will become from thoughts of your troubles.

Years later I discovered the true benefits of this whilst attending an Integrated Science Course with one of Hay House's best-selling authors, Dr David Hamilton PhD. Training with David has had a profound effect not only on my work, but on my life. Everything he taught only reinforced my absolute and definite belief that drugs are not the answer to our emotional problems.

It became clearly evident that we can change the way we feel dramatically through simple acts of kindness and compassion. Immersed in science, I discovered the benefits of kindness. Knowing that kindness caused a release of oxytocin, which had many health and happiness benefits, excited me. Could it also be that compassionate people had a healthier, more responsive inflammatory tool, the vagus nerve? It appeared to be so. Filled with knowledge and curiosity, my mind was alive with new thoughts and possibilities. A whole new world had opened up and I remember wondering how much longer we would all live if we all showed more kindness. I considered the concept of 'pro-kindness' instead of 'anti-bullying' education in schools. Why weren't children being taught this? I left the course days later on fire, eager to share my knowledge. It was bursting out of me. I knew that people needed to know this stuff. It could change so many lives. Just a few days later, the universe decided to test my learnings by delivering me Tom.

Whilst out shopping, laden with bags, my husband and I decided to look for a small romantic restaurant in which to have lunch. Not able to find anywhere that romantic, we settled on a small back-street pub which seemed particularly quiet, giving us ample opportunity to talk together. We sat and were handed menus before placing our orders for food, and awaited our drinks. We began to talk and out of the corner of my eye, I suddenly became aware of the elderly gentleman sat in the corner alone, with his old, hessian shopping bag.

I noticed how frail he seemed, as he picked up his walking stick, his bag and his pint and started to head in our direction. Knowing exactly what was about to happen, I saw my husband tense and I felt an uneasiness in my stomach, dreams of our romantic lunch together rapidly slipping away.

Reaching our table, he put his pint down and explained that his table was wobbly and that his drink kept spilling before delivering the question we knew was headed our way. "Would I be able to sit with you?" he asked. The other empty tables must all have been wobbly too.

At that moment, I knew that what I was about to say would not only have a dramatic impact on our supposedly romantic lunch, but a dramatic impact on this man's day. He won, because flooded with compassion (and avoiding eye contact with my husband) I replied, "Of course," and patted the seat for him to sit down. The waitress, having witnessed the situation, walked over and whispered into my ear, "I will ask him to move if you like." "Thank you," I replied, and then speaking from my heart, "but it's fine."

He introduced himself as Tom and then proceeded to share his story. He spoke about his life, and told us that he wanted to work on steam trains from a very young age. Upon applying for his first job, he told us that he said, "I ain't got no qualifications or those levels or whatever you call them, but what I do have is a spirit level, and a high one at that." He told us that he got the job and proceeded to pull an old crumpled black-and-white photograph from his pocket so that he could show us 'his train'. He told us that he would cook his breakfast on the coal shovel in the fire of the train every morning, and took delight in witnessing our interest. He spoke with sadness in his voice as he shared memories of days with his wife, who had passed away years ago. We watched him re-ignite his soul with stories about his children, and his grandchildren. And we listened intently as he looked us right in the eyes, and told us to make the most of every minute, of every day, of every year. We felt warm inside listening to his words. My husband and I didn't get our romantic lunch together, but what we got was so much more.

CHANGING ROOM TIP

Make People Feel Important

"Pretend that everyone you meet has a sign around his or her neck that says 'Make Me Feel Important'. Not only will you succeed in sales, you will succeed in life."

Mary Kay Ash

This is such a simple way to express kindness, but without doubt very powerful. Everyone wants to feel valued and special, and that they have a place in the world. You can make people feel special by giving your presence and your words. Every single day, you walk past people who feel invisible and who need your words more than you will ever know. Whilst visiting a friend in an elderly care home, I would often talk to the other residents sitting nearby. Noticing a gentleman sat alone in the corner on the other side of the room, I wandered over to make conversation. The words that I heard left me stunned. "Do you know, no one ever talks to me?" he said. "Because I can feed and dress myself, no one ever talks to me." The emotion that I felt at that moment still drives me today to make as many people as I can in the time that I have here on earth feel important.

My biggest discovery is that kindness is very contagious. I believe that inwardly we all know what to do and how to live, which is why we are easily infected by the kindness of others. The following experience is a very memorable example:

Following a hospital appointment for a hip check up, I returned to the ticket payment machine in the car park. An elderly couple were having trouble getting the machine to accept their coins and I watched them try repeatedly. Seeing that it was causing distress, I offered to pay the £2.60 with my debit card, which was what I was intending to do with my own ticket.

The elderly couple looked at each other. The little old lady replied, "Well, if you don't mind?" They then proceeded to try to give me £2.60 in cash, which I declined. Sensing their confusion I said, "I'd love it to be a random act of kindness, people have helped me in the past and it would give me great pleasure to help you right now." Suddenly, the growing queue of complaining people behind us fell silent as the elderly lady took my hand in hers. She looked me straight in the eye and into my soul and said, "I wish you a truly beautiful life, and all the luck in the world, you are very kind indeed."

The car park attendant then arrived and I was absolutely astounded at the people behind us, who had previously been voicing their dissatisfaction at having to wait. The car park attendant apologised profusely, and to my amazement a gentleman in the queue said, "Not a problem at all, we know you do your best." Others then joined in giving the car park attendant compliments. The long queue of people began smiling and laughing together. I joined the party and recognised that I was having a lot of fun too, with a small group of totally random strangers. My intention didn't quite work out as planned, as the car park attendant actually needed to use the elderly couple's coins to test that the machine was working after being reset (it was, and their ticket was returned to them).

Before they went on their way, the elderly lady took my arm and held it tight, looked into my eyes once more, and said, "Thank you, thank you." It was a beautiful moment, and one that I hold close to my heart. The experience touched me deeply and I wanted others to benefit from my learning. I posted the story on my business Facebook page, and later read this comment from a lovely lady called Lindsey Hibbert:

"I read your update earlier about Treliske car park... I have since done some acts of kindness myself (not so random!) but to let people know that I care... I left a bunch of flowers at my mother's door, I got a lovely cake from the baker's for an older gent that I clean for and another couple I look after are away (as her mum is very poorly) and I did two lots of her washing and hung it out for her. I then saw a little dish that she would love and filled it with some chocolate that her husband would love... and although I have not seen any of these people... they have no idea what I've done (even though small gestures)... it does give you a warm feeling inside."

Later that day I received a message from author David Hamilton PhD, asking if he could share my post on his Facebook page. My one simple story about kindness probably spread to thousands of people. How many acts of kindness were carried out as a result, I often wonder?

Kindness is like liquid gold that flows between us through selfless acts. Opportunities to create beautiful moments and memories like this are available to us every single day, yet we often fail to recognise them. When I teach workshops, the topic of kindness also creates a silence in the room in which you could hear a pin drop. Always. The strongest reaction that I experienced was with a very large group of teenagers. Whilst delivering a happiness workshop, I asked the participants to bring to mind the last time that they were kind, for no other reason than to help another. The alpha males in the group, who had moments before been showing their dominance through their volume of their words and their body language, sat frozen to their seats, silenced. From the stage I witnessed countless wide eyes deep in shock at their personal revelation. But it's not just teenagers who forget to be kind, we all do. We get caught up in the chaos of busy living and lose sight of what's important. You may have feelings just like those teenagers right now as you sit and read this book, and experience your own revelation. These feelings are your power. This knowledge is your strength. Use both your strength and your power to make kindness an essential part of your being, not just now but forever. The more you give, the more you will receive in so many ways. Giving to others will make you feel truly alive and connected to your soul.

You deserve nothing less than to feel like this. Here are some ideas to help you give your attention to others, and spread kindness galore!

- *Bake a cake for a neighbour*

- *Spend time talking with an elderly person (visiting an elderly care home is one of the most rewarding experiences you will ever have)*
- *Drop a small anonymous gift to someone that you know*
- *Write a letter or send a card letting someone know what you love most about them*
- *Offer to pay for someone's coffee in a coffee shop*
- *Send someone a book you know they will love in the post*
- *Offer to look after small children, to give a parent a rest*
- *Compliment a stranger, and mean it from the heart*
- *Send someone a bunch of flowers, simply for being themselves*

By being kind you will feel happier, it's been proven time and time again. One particular study[3] asked people to carry out five acts of kindness, one day a week for six weeks. They were asked to vary the acts as much as possible. After six weeks they were much happier then the control group who had made no effort to be kind. Kindness is a free, no-prescription-necessary anti-depressant. Side effects include smiling and heartfelt warmth.

---

[3] S. Lyubomirsky, C. Tkach, and K.M. Sheldon, 'Pursuing Sustained Happiness Through Random Acts Of Kindness and Counting One's Blessings: Testing of Two Six-Week Interventions', Department of Psychology, University Of California, Riverside, unpublished data, 2004.

> *Simple and unexpected acts of kindness can literally change your life, and help to change the lives of others too. I love that. What are you going to do to learn to love it too?*

Having been on the receiving end of so much kindness, I returned home from my NLP course, spirit fed and watered. I felt hugely empowered, bursting at the seams with new knowledge. Within a day of my return, empowerment was temporarily overshadowed by frustration. Living in the country and unable to drive made me feel like a caged animal. I begged my husband for a mobility scooter from his shop to get out and about. Using the scooter gave me a new sense of freedom. I also found therapy in throwing my crutches on the back and zooming along the pavements with the wind in my fine wispy bits of hair. I enjoyed it so much that I was out every day, flitting around the streets, going to family and friends for coffee. Unfortunately some friends didn't know that I had discovered this freedom and still turned up at my home, expecting me to be lying in bed, feeling sorry for myself. (I apologise to those who turned up bearing gifts, but at the time I was having far too much fun out on the streets.) I was slightly limited mobility wise but I was fully dressed without my wig, full of confidence and positivity, and I wanted to go out and show the world. Sod the lack of my hair on my head and the lack of mobility in my hips. Yes, stuff happens and it knocks you down and strips you right back. But I'm here, I've bounced back and I'm living from my heart.

CHANGING ROOM TIP

Don't Be A Sheep, Be Unique

When I first rode the mobility scooter, I felt as if I stood out like a sore thumb. On my first trip out I kept my eyes to the floor, hoping to become invisible so that people I knew wouldn't notice me. This didn't really work out because I collided with a lamp post. I came to the conclusion that it would be much braver, and safer, to sit tall and face my fear. I bore the brunt of many jokes from my friends and received many comments from strangers. People in my community were curious as to why the 'lady who six weeks ago had a head full of hair and could walk' was bombing around the streets not far from bald on a mobility scooter.

Maybe I didn't conform to society's expectations following a very large and pretty brutal operation, but by now, I simply didn't care. I'd given up trying to fit in, because by now I'd kind of figured out that I never would. It simply wasn't possible. I started to have far more fun doing what I loved, guided by my heart. For the first time in my life, I truly embraced standing out. It was fun to be different.

In my experience, the people that have the confidence to stand out are often the ones that are not only the most successful, but the happiest. This is because they are doing what they love to do, having followed their heart instead of their head. Guided by their own thoughts instead of those of others, they live the life they want.

We often stray from the life that we want because we try to conform. We try to fit in. We think that to be beautiful we have to be a size 8, with spectacular cheekbones and dazzling white teeth. People inject themselves with Botox to conform to society's perception that wrinkle free is how we are meant to be. People work five days a week, because they have learnt from others (who also work five days a week), that it's the 'norm'. (My husband and I broke that rule and both work a four-day week, we would never, ever go back.) There are so many rules by which we as a society unconsciously live our lives. These rules can restrict our lives, and our happiness. Don't be afraid to break the rules. Tear them up and make your own! Why try to fit in when you were born to stand out?

Don't be a sheep, be unique!

After a brief 'holiday', having explored every road and pavement on my scooter to the point of starting to burn through the tyres, I decided I really should go back to work. I started coaching again, gradually integrating my NLP learnings, and began to recognise my true power as a coach. Not only was I using knowledge gained from my training, I was using knowledge gained through my own personal experiences. A month later I returned to complete the final modules of the NLP course, and qualified as a practitioner. I began using a huge amount of NLP in my work, and found that with these skills I could help practically anyone that came through my door with any issue, including phobias. And it was a phobia which led to my final 'dress of confidence' when I appeared live on television.

FINDING SELF LOVE

One particular day whilst flicking through the television channels, I came across a programme called 'A Life Coach Less Ordinary', featuring Nik and Eva Speakman. What totally captivated me was their absolute and undeniable belief that anyone could change. I watched as they helped people overcome their fears and phobias, changing people's lives right before my eyes. As I watched my spirit soared and all the pieces of the jigsaw puzzle suddenly fitted together. The picture was clear and powerful. For the very first time I became aware of my similar absolute and undeniable belief that anyone could change. Alopecia, chronic fatigue syndrome and hip dysplasia had given me walking, talking proof.

Knowing that I would soon be working with clients and their phobias, I felt it necessary to overcome my own. For years I had been carrying the burden of molluscophobia, an extreme fear of snails. The presence of a snail could reduce me to an uncontrollable and quivering wreck within seconds. Have you ever experienced sheer terror? I would feel it on a regular basis. Though it may seem trivial to many, it had a huge effect on my day-to-day life. I avoided going out into the garden when it had been raining at all costs. Parents' evenings at school were my worst nightmare, because in the classroom was a glass tank housing not only snails, but giant snails. A snail that appeared unexpectedly on a window at home would make me cry and shake uncontrollably. Even my husband suffered. One evening as I walked into the kitchen, approaching the light switch, my husband entered the room from the other side. Holding out his hand, he said, "I've got something for you." In the darkness I saw a small round shape. Reaching near-hysteria in seconds and with huge force I thumped his hand away. Unfortunately I hit him so hard that his hand hit his head. He yelled in pain, and I ran as fast as I could to the bedroom and locked myself in sobbing. Not only was my husband hurt, he was also very confused. All he had done was try to offer me a Malteser. (In my defence, I'd had a bad experience whilst working in a fast food restaurant in my teens. Another member of staff had offered me their box of chicken nuggets. I sat in the staff room grateful for their generosity and ready to tuck in, opened the lid, and looked in absolute horror at the multiple sets of moving eyes on stalks. I screamed hysterically and ran away as far as I could, as fast as I could. Aware of my fear, my friend had thought it would be an amusing prank.) Where this phobia had originated from, I had no idea. There were many pictures in family photograph albums of me surrounded by snails in glass jars as a young child. (I once loved to collect them.) I remembered playing snail races on a concrete slope outside my house with friends. I genuinely could not understand where and when this irrational fear had arisen. Having the knowledge and tools to help others overcome their fears added to my frustration, and I knew I needed someone else to guide me through the process.

Having been inspired by Nik and Eva Speakman, I decided to find out more about their services on their website. Within just a few minutes my fingers happily tapped away on the keys enquiring as to how much it would cost to have them help me. To have my phobia cured and to meet the people that had inspired me beyond belief would be a dream come true!

I was amazed by the rapid response, and was asked whether I would like to book an appointment. After a brief discussion with my husband about the cost, it became clear that it wasn't something that we could really afford at the time. Frustrated, I tried to let the idea go, but it refused to disappear and gnawed away at me. How could I make it happen? A week later, a spectacular gift from the universe arrived in my inbox in the form of an email.

This is an exact copy of the words that I saw in front of my eyes:

"Hi Maria

The producers of Nik and Eva's live Motivational Monday Breakfast Show are always looking for people to come on the show with strange phobias, so I have run your story by them. If they agree then you would have to be at the studio in Manchester for 7.30am. I am just awaiting their feedback and if they agree, a date which would be in about 4 weeks."

I had been offered a free phobia cure, a television appearance and I would get to meet the two people that had inspired me so much. Floating ecstatically in a moment of euphoria, I messaged back to say "I agree." It really was a no brainer. Had I unconsciously sent a message to the universe? Were angels watching over me? I wasn't sure but was beginning to strongly believe that anything was possible if you wanted it enough.

CHANGING ROOM LESSON
Anything Is Possible

Anything is possible. I've come to realise that when we put our minds to it, practically anything is possible. We are only limited by what we believe is possible. Our actions either empower or restrict us depending on what we believe. Many years ago, I met an old school friend who was at the time working in a D.I.Y shop. Recognising each other, we began talking and it became evident that he was very unhappy in his job. "That's life, though," he said, "It's about accepting your unhappiness to pay the bills." His thoughts about possibility were restricting his life. He didn't choose to look for a job that would make him happy, because he didn't think it was possible.

What do you feel about the possibilities in your life? Are you boxing yourself in with your thoughts? What would it be like if you chose today to believe that anything is possible? What would you do differently? What impact would this have on your choices, your actions, your life, and ultimately your happiness?

Use the exercise below to create insight and opportunity.

If anything were possible I would:

1.

2.

3.

4.

5.

6.

7.

8.

9.

10.

What would you need to start believing to open your mind to these possibilities?

There are those who dream of what they'll never have, and those who dream of what they are going to get.

Which will you choose to be?

Flying to Manchester to appear on the TV show, excitement mixed with apprehension as I considered that I might be exposed to my worst fear in just a few hours. Still relying on crutches to support me, I made the decision to leave them behind. I hadn't informed the television crew that I used crutches, being worried that they would see me as a live

TV health and safety risk! A short time later, I found myself sat in the studio talking to Nik and Eva before being filmed. I discovered very quickly that they were both humble and beautiful people. I was guided on to the 'Breakfast sofa' a short while later, and Nik and Eva questioned me about my fear in front of Manchester television viewers. Never in a million years did I expect them to reach behind the sofa and put on the coffee table a plate of crawling slimy snails. Eyes on stalks, slime, crunchy shells served up on a platter, just for me.

Fear enveloped me, tears filled my eyes as a million exit strategies filled my mind. My initial thought was to jump over the sofa and run but my recent hip operation was a concern. My thoughts went to the TV producers... would they be furious if I disappeared? Knowing that my friends were watching the programme became added pressure... I decided that it would be better to summon every bit of strength possible and face my fear, rather than face the humiliation for years to come. Sweat began to pour down my brow as I physically began to shake. My heart racing, I tried to avoid looking like a complete fruitcake by not looking at my offerings. If the plate came any closer, I would be gone, very quickly and a very long way away. Sod the hip.

Sensing my anxiety, they removed the snails and Nik and Eva set to work with me off air. Just a short time later, for the first time in 25 years I not only touched, but picked up a snail on camera. Every ounce of fear had disappeared, and I was left feeling remarkably calm and astounded by the change in my feelings.

The full extent of my progress became very clear a short time later when the YouTube video of my TV appearance went live. Yes, it was liberating to be free from the fear of snails, but watching the video was enlightening. I had just appeared on TV without a wig, a million hair grips restraining my wispy hair and covering my bald patches. And just a few short weeks after a nine-hour hip operation. My biggest revelation was that I really didn't care what other people thought of my appearance, and the fact that my wispy hair probably looked quite a mess hadn't even crossed my mind. Never in my life had I been so unconcerned with other people's thoughts or opinions. Yes, my phobia had been cured, yes I'd met Nik and Eva, but it was far more than that. It was undeniable proof that I'd returned to my roots by losing my roots. I'd let go of all that I thought I was, and become who I was always destined to be. The light that pierced my soul, filled me from top to toe, and made me smile. I knew at that moment that I needed to spend the rest of my life sharing my light, helping others to find their smile too.

CHANGING ROOM TIP
Learn To Love You

You were born full of self-love, full of yourself, and you deserve nothing less. Not once did you question at twelve months old if your bottom looked too big in a nappy! Never did you think that you were a failure when you fell over time and time again learning to walk. Never did you wonder if people would like you as you tottered around on chubby legs at the age of two years! Never did you doubt your own ability to live an exceptional life.

Through childhood and into our teens we make sense of the world in the best way possible. We use our best judgement to interpret our experiences, and understand ourselves and the world around us. A lack of knowledge or resources, however, often leads to us wrongly interpreting situations. This starts to strip away our layers of self-love.

For example:

"He was unfaithful to me," unconsciously interpreted as "this must mean I'm not worth loving."

"My parents split up," unconsciously interpreted as "this must mean that I'm not enough to be loved." (Very common.)

"I have no hair," unconsciously interpreted by the author as "no one will ever be able to love me, so how can I love myself?"

What I'd like you to do right now, is to write on an A4 piece of paper in large letters:

'I LOVE ME'

Do it even if you don't believe this statement. Do it right now.

Look at the words you have written and notice how you feel inside. Pick up the piece of paper and slowly tear it into eight pieces. (I'm not joking, rip it up.) Lay the pieces on a table in front of you, and notice that what you have been doing unconsciously over the years is tearing yourself to pieces. How does this make you feel?

This is not the end of the exercise, because you are not meant to be in bits. I want you to find some tape, and stick all of these pieces back together, because you can heal. What you are looking at when those words have been reunited is yours for the taking.

I'd like you to start helping yourself by practising these thoughts below:

1. *You do not have to look like a supermodel to love yourself. Appearance is just a shell to carry your spirit and soul. You do, however, have the right to have a lovely, pretty, or handsome shell. If you want to treat yourself to a manicure or hair appointment on a regular basis then do it. Looking after and nurturing yourself strengthens positive self-belief.*

2. *Accept that you are enough, just as you are. What would it be like if you stopped comparing yourself to others? What difference would this make to your life? It's 100% certain that you can never be like anybody else. Within your brain you have your own networks of neural pathways, formed by millions of connections based on your life learnings and experiences. Therefore, it's impossible for anyone to be exactly like you, so there is little point in trying to be like them! You are beautifully unique so embrace and celebrate your differences!*

3. *Recognise that there is no such thing as failure, only feedback. If things don't go to plan then see it as an opportunity to learn and grow. If you didn't get a job*

> *following an interview, it doesn't mean that you are not*
> *good enough! It could just mean that you need to brush*
> *up on interview techniques. If a relationship ends, don't*
> *allow it to take away self-love, simply see it as one step*
> *closer to a relationship that does work.*
>
> 4. *Focus on your strengths and achievements. What are*
>   *you proud of? What have you achieved? Make lists and*
>   *add to them on a regular basis! Focus on what makes*
>   *you feel good.*
>
> 5. *Surround yourself with people who make you feel*
>   *amazing. It's difficult to rise when you have others*
>   *wanting to keep you in a cage. Look for the people who*
>   *already fly and they will help you spread your wings.*

Following my television appearance, I continued wig-less with my coaching career and continued to embrace the real me; who I had become, and who I finally believed I was meant to be. My hip recovered and I could eventually walk without a limp and again wear my favourite chunky heeled brown leather winter boots, which I loved. My hair was growing very slowly, and although having alopecia didn't emotionally destroy me anymore, I still dreamt of beautiful shiny locks. Knowing that my hair probably wasn't going to grow a foot overnight, I needed to find another way to *make it happen*. The idea of hair extensions seemed appealing, and not knowing if it was even possible in amongst the weird uneven re-growth on my head, I began making some calls. I rang ten hairdressers in total, but none of them were interested for fear of making my condition worse. They were afraid of me and my patchy scalp. About to give up, I realised that I hadn't called a hairdresser's called Strawberry Blondes, which was in a town called Hayle, a few miles away. Taking a deep breath, I decided to give it one last shot. I listened to the phone ring on the other end, pre-empting the conversation that I would be likely to have yet again with a random hairdresser afraid of being sued.

But when the telephone was answered, I immediately sensed a very different reaction. The salon owner, Sue Crew, took the time to listen to my needs and asked me to pop down to see her, so that she could take a look. A day later I found myself sat in her salon, which was a strange and unfamiliar experience for someone who had not stepped into a hairdresser's for 14 years. Sue gently examined my hair and my scalp. Immediately I warmed to her vibrant personality and her positive 'make it happen' attitude. It became apparent that she understood how much it would mean to me to have proper hair. She agreed to 'give hair extensions a go', with regular checks to ensure that they weren't making my condition any worse. I informed her that I would take full responsibility, and that as I'd spent the last 14 years with virtually no hair, she couldn't possibly make it any worse. A week later, I walked out of her salon feeling on top of the world, with long, glossy, beautiful brown hair. Returning to my car, I sat and looked in the mirror, took a deep breath and, overloaded with uncontrollable emotion, I sobbed. I cried and cried, then cried some more. The outside of me now matched the inside. I took a selfie on my mobile phone and sent it to my husband. What on earth would he think or say? Later that day on my return home, I found out. He simply stared at me curiously and then announced that he quite liked the new look. His slow reaction led me to believe that seeing me with hair was quite a shock! For the next week I found myself looking in any mirror or reflection available, enjoying every single beautiful new moment of the new 'me'. Who would have guessed that an eleventh phone call could have resulted in such joy, gratitude and euphoria? Fourteen years waiting for hair that was attached to my head. Fourteen very long years. I couldn't have had it any earlier though, it simply wasn't possible. Until then, I hadn't learnt enough.

CHANGING ROOM TIP
Keep Banging On Doors Until One Opens

If you want something badly enough, then knock on enough doors until you get it. If you hear the word "no", then just keep going until you hear a "yes". I've found the best rewards in life are the ones that I've worked hardest for. Being naked we have to dig deep, and when we dig deep we find strength that we didn't know existed. Long term, we become less afraid of rejection because we've already been there. We become braver because we've had to be brave. We ask for what we want and we keep asking because we are stronger. We learn to love ourselves. We know who we are meant to be. We know we deserve what we ask for.

What are you missing out on in your life as a result of having given up?

Which doors do you have in front of you right now that you could knock on?

What help do you need to get you through?

What could you do to ask for that help?

What boundaries could you break through to get that help?

When you're naked, your strength is easier to find. With everything else stripped away, it's nearer the surface. It's closer than you think. It just needs a way to get out and express itself, and you yourself are the way. Reach into your soul and allow your strength to emerge. Bring what you have inside, out.

HAPPINESS IS ABOUT BEING CONFIDENT WITH WHO YOU ARE, STANDING TALL AND PROUD IN YOUR OWN SKIN.

IT'S ABOUT KNOWING THAT YOU CAN CHOOSE TO ADD CLOTHES, HAIR COLOURINGS, MAKE-UP, OR TATTOOS IF YOU WANT THEM.

BUT YOU DON'T RELY ON THEM, BECAUSE THE HAPPINESS THAT YOU FIND AS A RESULT OF NAKEDNESS CANNOT BE REMOVED OR TAKEN AWAY.

RISING HIGHER

Having been rebuilt from the inside out (in more ways than one), two years later I was challenged yet again. I began experiencing extreme pain in the hip that had been operated on. The limp returned as did the sleepless nights. The only option left was to have it replaced at the age of 37. One surgeon refused to do the operation because I was 'too young': he was concerned that the life span of hip replacements would cause me major problems long term. I knocked on another door, and the next surgeon agreed to operate after recognising that my quality of life was deteriorating due to the pain. My fitness career was taken from my life yet again. (How many times?!!) The operation was a success, and I was reunited with my two shiny aluminium friends who supported me once again for over six weeks. I'd lost my hip but I stood (albeit a little crooked for a while) smiling, with a growing sense of new opportunity coming my way. Though coaching had become my main career, I still loved the buzz of teaching fitness. Sat in my practice room every day with coaching clients was exceptionally rewarding and truly fed my soul, but I didn't physically move much. Teaching physical fitness gave me balance, and made up for so much sitting down during the day.

My surgeon had informed me that following my hip replacement, I needed to be careful with regards to the exercise that I undertook, advising me to avoid impact activities to prolong the life of the joint.

Refusing to be beaten, I questioned the purpose of having a piece of my body removed. What lesson was I meant to learn from this? It didn't take me long to figure it out. I'd start to teach people wanting an easier exercise class, the majority being the more 'mature' generation, especially people with hip replacements. Yes, I shared my story yet again with the local newspapers in order to generate interest, and took great delight in using my experiences to inspire others. A new, beautiful, shiny silver lining.

If the personal development world could be compared to the deep blue sea, I was still swimming every day. Any chance I could find I'd be in the water, immersing myself in new learnings: reading, studying, attending motivational seminars, and surrounding myself with people who strived to be the absolute best that they could be. I added to my tribe by connecting with positive people from all over the world. I fire-walked with hundreds of others at 'Unleash The Power Within' with Tony Robbins, twice. I immersed myself in more training. I spent time with happiness experts and some of the world's most highly regarded life coaches. I travelled and attended events all over the UK as often as I could to feed my soul and fuel my mind. I got as much from the people as I did from the events. Being surrounded by people who lived at a higher level was having a profound and very positive effect on my happiness. I wanted to share my knowledge more and more with others. The universe must have been aware of my intention, as I became increasingly sought after for speaking events. The difference that I could make to people's lives simply by sharing my story and my learnings astounded me. But I loved it. And I wanted to do it more and more.

CHANGING ROOM TIP

Who You Spend Time With Is Who You Become

The people that I have spent time with throughout my journey have massively influenced my outcome and where I am today in my life. Very early on I discovered that spending time around people who wanted to better their lives had a dramatic impact not only on my thoughts and behaviour, but on the results I got in life. Throughout my varied training, I became surrounded by people with very positive attitudes. This fuelled my confidence and knowledge and made me more like them. I'm reminded of the famous quote:

"You are the average of the people you spend the most time with."

Jim Rohn

Who do you spend the most time with? If you want to take your life up a level, then you need to ensure that you have enough of the right people in your life to help you rise. If you haven't, then you need to go and seek them out! If you want to be free from negative thoughts, then you need to spend time with people with a positive attitude. You need to be around the appropriate brain trainers. Think about what you would do if you wanted to improve your tennis or running performance. Would you go and choose someone to coach you who wasn't very good at the sport? Absolutely not. You would seek out an experienced professional. To get happy, you need to seek out happiness professionals; those that already have and maintain exceptional happiness!

Trying to climb with others holding you down is exhausting and difficult. To fly free, you need to be surrounded by others who will lift you. It can be useful to think of people as Super Stylers, Style Sources, Style Supporters, or Style Squashers!

Super Stylers: These people will see your true potential, and want you to fulfil it! They can see the absolute best version of you in their mind, and they know what you need to feel alive and thrive. They challenge you when you say "I can't" and they speak with absolute conviction when reminding you of your strengths and talents. Super Stylers are 'make it happen' people, and they love nothing more than to see you re-dressed with spectacular happiness. Evidence of this can be seen in their use of strong and positive language.

Style Sources: These people have many friends and acquaintances. Style Sources can be compared to 'Google on legs'. They seem to have an infinite amount of knowledge and connections. They have the ability to recognise what you need, and take great pleasure in introducing you to their contacts to help you succeed. As a result, they offer you the opportunity to experiment with your own beautiful and unique style, until you find the right combination of things that make you happy. Their language is also positive and strong, and knowing that they can help you only fuels their excitement.

Style Supporters: Supporters are reliable and grounded people. They are great listeners and steadfast in their advice. Being in their company makes you feel reassured and calm. They may not have all the solutions, or know what action you need to take, but their support is unwavering. They have the ability to reduce your stress levels by offering their ears. You are then in a better place to see clearly, and find your own answers. They listen more than they talk, and their empathy is evident in their words. They know that you deserve to be happy in your own skin, and want the best for you.

Style Squashers: These people do just that, they try to squash your style. To stand dressed with happiness, it will be necessary to make changes in your life. Style Squashers will try to stop you changing. They will try to keep you dressed as you are for one of two reasons:

1. *They are unhappy themselves, and afraid of change. They want to keep you feeling like them so they feel more normal.*

2. *They may feel that your change may impact them negatively. A son who wants to travel to 'find himself' may find his mother 'squashing' his style and his plans with her words. Her intention is to keep him at home because she would miss him too much.*

Style Squashers are not bad people; it's highly likely that they haven't found the right help themselves or are lacking in knowledge. As a result, they will often react negatively if you speak about hopes and dreams and change. They will make it very difficult for you to change, and will try to influence you to stay just as you are. Their language is often negative, and can be emotionally draining.

My own personal research has taught me that generally people have more Style Supporters than any other of the categories in their lives. Style Squashers are also very common, but you need to limit the time you spend with these people. Style Sources and Super Stylers tend to be the rarest, but they are the most important. You need to spend as much time as possible with Style Sources and Super Stylers. If you don't have any, then open your eyes and look for them. You will know immediately when you have been in the presence of either of them; you will feel as if you have been sprinkled with sunshine. Connect with them and maintain the connections because they want to share their shine. They want to see you living with happiness and joy. Only when surrounded by positive people will you maintain positive change within your life.

Identify the people in your life right now by category. This will create a greater awareness and allow you to see the changes that may be necessary.

My Super Stylers:

My Style Sources:

My Style Supporters:

My Style Squashers:

What have you learnt from this exercise?

Who do you need more or less of in your life?

As you seek more people to enhance your life, it's very important to keep an open mind with regards to age. When we spend time with people of varying ages we learn more and potentially increase our happiness. Some of my most valued friends are between 65 and 80 years. More mature generations are often very happy and truly appreciate life. They have high spirit levels and the power to create smiles and much laughter. They also have the ability and the time to have deep, heartfelt conversations and as a result offer exceptional advice. (I deeply value these people in my life.)

At the other end of the scale, I find myself inspired by the young. They do what they want and ask for what they want, and spend time around people that they like. They find excitement in muddy puddles, and beauty within nature. They speak from their hearts and say how they feel and accept nothing less than happiness.

Instead of looking for a suitable age, look for a suitable 'spirit'. Make it your mission to become a 'super spirit seeker' today!

Spilling over with new knowledge, living with passion leaking through my pores, I knew I needed to find more ways to help others. I had trained further and reached NLP Trainer level by this time, which had further fuelled my confidence and my passion for motivational speaking. As a speaker I continued to share my story and my learnings with large groups of people. I began to thrive on the changes that I could instigate in others with my words. One of the highlights of my life was when a 90-year-old man approached me following a talk, hugged me, and cried. He told me that his whole life, and everything he had been through had suddenly made sense. I knew at that very moment I wasn't reaching enough people. It was then that I knew I needed to reach more people another way. It had to be a book. This book. I hoped and prayed that amongst shopping, washing, being a mum, a life coach, a fitness instructor and a wife, I would somehow find extra time to write. I knew with all my heart that I had to share my story more widely.

After two years of praying, my solution appeared when my one remaining good hip became painful and was diagnosed with arthritis. Knowing that this hip too would need to be replaced in the future, I eventually chose to let go of my fitness career for good. It was an emotional time, saying goodbye to something that had been such a huge part of my life, my soul, and my being for so many years. Yes, I cried, and the last class that I ever taught was emotionally one of the toughest. As hard as it was, I also felt strangely empowered. It didn't feel like something had been taken away yet again, it felt as if I'd let it go.

CHANGING ROOM TIP

Letting Go Makes Room For More Good Stuff

"Some people believe holding on and hanging in there are signs of great strength. However, there are times when it takes much more strength to know when to let go, and then do it."

Ann Lander

It can often be harder to let go than it is to hold on. Nevertheless, letting go of thoughts or behaviours that no longer serve us, can be not only beneficial, but empowering. We know when we need to let go because we begin to hurt, and the pain we feel doesn't go away. It's a strong sign that something needs to change.

Many years ago, my son owned a pair of bright blue trainers that he loved so, so much. As he grew, so did his feet, and his shoes began to 'pinch' his feet causing him pain. He refused to accept that he needed new trainers, and was determined to keep wearing them. The soles began to come away, letting in dirt and water, and they became so uncomfortable that he eventually decided to let go and let me buy him new shoes. Did he miss his old ones? Not at all; as soon as he put the new trainers on his feet he realised that they were far more comfortable, and he could run a lot further in them.

Your shoes can be compared to your beliefs about your current situation. What beliefs are you 'wearing' that are preventing you going further? (I initially believed that by letting go of my fitness classes, I would be letting go of a part of me. After realising that they were part of my journey, not part of me, it was easier to say farewell.)

What I came to realise is this:

1. *If it's possible to let go of something, then it's not part of who we are.*

2. *Letting go of something doesn't mean that the good memories disappear. It makes them more important.*

3. *Letting go is scary, yes, but it's even scarier not to let go and to stay stuck.*

Working through personal challenges or adversity, it's highly likely that you will have to let go of something at some point, whether it be an emotion or a behaviour. We may fear losing what we have known, but letting go opens us up to new possibilities, within a wonderful new world.

Do you need to let go of blame or hurt?

Do you need to let go of a relationship, or a job?

Do you need to let go of bad habits, or behaviours?

What could you let go of NOW that would make the biggest difference to your life?

There's no better time than now. Tick tock. Time's up.

Letting Go Of Something Physical
Ask yourself, "What will happen if I keep this thing?" Then, ask yourself, "What will happen if I let go?" Your soul will begin to speak and guide you in the form of a feeling.

Letting Go Of An Emotion Or Feeling
Ask yourself the above questions, and hear the words from your soul. Then, do one of the following:

- Write the emotion or feeling on a piece of paper, make a fire, and watch it turn to ash.

- Write it on a stone, and toss it out to sea.

- Write it on a gas balloon, and watch in peace as it floats away.

- *Find a small object that represents your emotion or feeling, and bury it in a tiny box in the garden. Plant a small bush or a tree on top to symbolise your growth. (There is a lovely red rose called 'Moment In Time', which seems highly appropriate.)*

The physical movement of watching a negative emotion disappear is a very empowering process. (I have used these techniques with group trainings, and such simple tools create very spiritual moments.)

CHANGING ROOM TIP
Create Your Vision

To help you let go, think about what you want your future to be. Record your answers to the questions below:

- *What do you want to be?*

- *Where do you want to be?*

- *What do you want to be doing?*

Looking at your answers, ask yourself, "Is it possible to have these things without letting go?" The chances are, you will realise that in order to create your desirable future, there are things you need to let go.

Creating a strong and compelling image of what you want in your future is a very powerful technique to increase your motivation. Imagine standing at the bottom of the mountain, trying to climb up to get away from your pain. On its own, this isn't enough and it's exhausting. It's like trying to climb an icy mountain wearing flip-flops. It's not going to happen.

When you create strong images of a desirable future, you create a vision of yourself standing at the top of the mountain. By imagining yourself at the top, you will create good feelings inside, just as if you were at the top! That vision creates a force that will help you rise. Pushing yourself up, aided by this force, not only doubles your motivation, but your power to move. It's like wearing crampons on an icy mountain and anchoring yourself to the top. The only way is up.

Keep sight of your goal, because it is strength for your soul.

HOLDING ON IS BELIEVING THAT THERE IS ONLY A PAST; LETTING GO IS KNOWING THAT THERE IS A FUTURE.

Daphne Rose Kingma

THE FINAL GIFT – REALIGNMENT

Having let go of my fitness career, my coaching career flourished. My worry that 'letting go' would leave a regrettable 'hole' had been laid to rest. New opportunities to expand in the field of coaching started to come in thick and fast. It was as if the universe knew what I needed. Through embracing these opportunities, I began to realise that every single part of my journey and every naked moment, had been turned around and put to good use. I continued to work with increasing numbers of clients, from all over the UK. I thrived on helping them find 'their outfit', their direction, and their purpose. I was coaching, running personal development workshops, and in demand as a motivational speaker. I took great delight in sharing my story with others, so that they may find their way to a happier future too. Never in a million years had I dreamt that I would find such fulfilment. Every day I awoke feeling excited about life, and about my purpose. Yes, I still had alopecia (cleverly disguised with hair extensions), one false hip and arthritis in the other, but nothing stopped me any more. I had developed a very strong belief that 'anything is possible' having been through so much, and I thrived on delivering that message to others, in any way, shape, or form. My thoughts and words were my tools.

My life was mapped out, I knew where I was going and I took steps every day. Our children, now all teenagers, were starting to find their own way in the world as they began to prepare for their futures. My husband and I too focused on our long-term goals and plans.

It was all planned: of course we would take great delight in seeing our offspring grow and explore, find love, and one day supply us with tiny footsteps again in the form of grandchildren, that was a given. But what else?

The rest of our dreams and desires came to light over regular coffees that we would grab together whenever we could. It didn't matter where we met (it was often a local café for ease), the conversation was always the same. We spoke about our future and what we wanted. And we spoke about plans for our shared greatest love: travel.

Yes, plans were made. One day we would holiday more, and travel more. We would explore more of France and Spain. We talked about going to India and more parts of Africa as we reflected on our learnings from our time in The Gambia. (We had been truly humbled by the happiness of the people who lived in such poverty.) We would get a camper van and explore the world. We would walk together more, and spend more quality time together. We would watch more movies, dine out, and have exciting adventures. Yes we would. Through my challenges, I had become an expert goal setter. Our plans were now firmly set in stone. I had stood naked and lost, in pits, at the bottom of many mountains and had become a happiness professional as a result. The importance of goal setting and life planning had been firmly integrated into my soul, spirit and my being. It had become as necessary as my morning cup of tea. Our lives would be nothing short of amazing.

What neither of us had anticipated was the grenade that dropped into our lives one Tuesday evening in 2013, which exploded and seemingly blew apart our plans before slamming us – both of us, this time – back into the changing room.

My husband had always had slightly unusual skin on his neck, appearing a little more wrinkly than the average person. It had never bothered him and it had certainly never bothered me; it was something that I grew to love about him, a quirky uniqueness, a stamp of individuality! Simply, by chance a nurse noticed this skin one day and politely mentioned that it should be investigated, refusing to give us any more information, in case we 'freaked out'.

Concerned, I began to trawl the internet, my husband oblivious to my research. Many doctors had seen and examined my husband over the years, and no one had ever noticed or mentioned this before. I searched the internet to no avail, so gave up and forgot all about it for a few weeks. Then, one Tuesday evening I had time to spare. The nurse's words still niggling, I tried searching again and again. An hour later I changed one key word, hit the search button, and a picture of a neck identical to my husband's appeared before my eyes. The wrinkling of the skin was apparently caused by a loss of elastic tissue. My eyes scanned the description; apparently it was a person with a condition called PXE. PXE? What the hell was PXE? It turned out to be a very rare genetic condition otherwise known as Pseudoxanthoma Elasticum, a systemic condition affecting the skin, eyes, and vascular systems. It was apparently an inherited disorder that caused elastic tissue to become mineralized within the body.

My eyes scanned the list of symptoms: skin lesions giving a 'cobblestone appearance', retinal disease and calcification of elastic fibres in the arteries. A sense of uneasiness filled me, as I thought back to the results of an X-ray my husband had on his hip a few years previously. The X-ray had shown that his hip was fine, but the results were accompanied by a very serious letter from the radiographer, 'highly concerned' by the very high levels of visible calcification in his arteries. His GP had acted on the advice of the radiographer and arranged various investigations, but nothing abnormal was found. It was concluded that it was just the way he was made.

Feeling a mild sense of panic, I passed the computer to my husband and asked him to look at the picture and read the symptoms. He agreed that there seemed to be quite a similarity and that he should visit the GP. I tried to put words such as 'devastating visual complications' to the back of my mind but they didn't want to sit there. Days later they were still all I could think about whilst waiting for the GP appointment.

It turned out that the GP had never even heard of PXE, but took our concerns seriously and referred my husband to a genetic specialist, who one month later examined my husband's neck and confirmed the diagnosis. Very confused as to what this actually meant, we sat and absorbed as much information as we could, trying to figure out whether we should be worried or not. We were told that as long as my husband didn't drink or smoke and stayed as healthy as possible, then he should be expected to live a normal life span. (Fortunately, he neither drank nor smoked.) The specialist seemed positive and upbeat, until we were about to leave his office, when we heard him say, "It's the eyes that you really need to be concerned about." I prayed that I had got it wrong, and was imagining the pity in his voice, when he mentioned sight loss. He tried to reassure us that no one with PXE ever goes completely and totally blind.

Apparently, there would always be peripheral vision. We left the office not really knowing how to feel, the words we had heard didn't seem to apply to us. After all, my husband had gone 44 years with no problems at all. What had changed? Seemingly nothing. But a week later my husband returned from the ophthalmology appointment that had been arranged. He looked shocked as he walked in the door. "What did they say?" I asked. "They looked me in the eye, and said, 'It's bad news I'm afraid.'" He had been informed that several 'angioid streaks' were visible, small breaks in the Bruch's membrane of the eye caused by mineralisation of this elastic-rich layer. Blood vessels leaking through these cracks could lead to degeneration of the area of central vision. He was told it was essential that he was monitored on a regular basis for the rest of his life.

My husband was a little unsettled but quickly appeared to put it to the back of his mind and return to normal life. It seemed to impact me more than him emotionally, which made me feel guilty. How could I feel so upset, when he could possibly suffer so much more? What right did I have to let it upset me? With time, the sense of uneasiness within me began to fade and eventually we both almost forgot about his diagnosis. After all, nothing had really changed. That is until just six months later, when my husband returned from work on January 5th.

His face as he walked in was ashen. He asked to speak to me in the kitchen, alone. He told me that he had started to lose the vision in one eye, and it had happened suddenly, that day. Witnessing his distress, I knew it must be serious; it took a lot to shake up my husband.

Weeks of emotional torture followed, for both of us. We knew that he had to be seen urgently by the eye department at our local hospital. We had been told there were injections that he may be able to have, that could possibly save his sight. A visit to eye casualty, followed by many appointments to see various ophthalmologists, resulted in feelings of absolute hopelessness and despair. For an injection to be given there had to be a visible bleed in the back of the eye but none could be found. My husband's sight continued to deteriorate in one eye. It became heart-breaking watching him squint to try and watch the television or work on his computer. He started randomly disappearing and I would find him lying in the bedroom alone with lights off and curtains drawn. He simply found it easier to stare at the dark than make sense of objects in the light. With a steely determination to help him I stayed strong in his company, silencing my screams of frustration and pain, watching the man that I loved start to lose his sight. My parents bore the brunt of my emotions as, needing to offload, I would turn up often on their doorstep in floods of tears. Open ears, a cup of tea, and hugs; I would then be able to get through another few days.

Our future plans, our dreams of travel and so much more, gone. Our lives had been turned upside down. The sights that we had planned to see, my husband may never see. And the absolute worst part was imagining what it would be like for him not to be able to drive; as long as I had known him driving and vehicles had been his passion. Would he ever see our children marry? Or the smiling faces of our grandchildren? I knew that these were negative thoughts, and that I should be trying to evict them from my mind. Unfortunately, there were reminders everywhere. One of the worst was when we were both standing on the side of the football pitch watching our youngest son play. My husband informed me that he couldn't see which one was our son anymore. Trying to stay upbeat he laughed, as his wife turned away to hide the pain in her heart and her tears behind sunglasses.

Because PXE is so incredibly rare, there is very little support. Most medical professionals still to this day are totally unfamiliar with it. Because PXE causes a hardening of arteries, my husband was referred to a cardiovascular specialist as a result of his diagnosis. The consultant admitted that he had 'Googled PXE' the night before my husband's appointment. We did however appreciate his honesty.

Our only help came from the PXE Facebook group, a forum where people from all over the world came together to help each other. Sat alone and crying in a crumpled heap on the dining room floor one day, I spoke online to a complete stranger in America. This lady's husband also had PXE and her strength and words that day helped me through. She advised us to keep going back to hospital, and keep shouting to be heard. It was 2014... we had the internet, we had people going into space, we had paraplegics walking in metal suits. How was it possible that a 44-year-old man was being left to lose his sight? Nobody seemed to care.

In desperation we called hospitals all over the UK, attempting to find extra help, with little success. Finally we called a lady suffering with PXE herself who had been known to help others, and she called our hospital on our behalf. We're not sure what she said, or whether it helped, but immediately after that we got an appointment with a consultant in the eye department, who was familiar with PXE. Co-incidentally he discovered that there was now a visible bleed and that my husband needed injections. Phew bloody phew. Tears of relief and joy flooded down my face as I heard his words.

These tears however, were replaced by tears of hysteria seconds later as we heard him say, "We may not be able to give you the injections because they have not been approved by the NHS for funding for your condition. They cost hundreds of pounds each and you are going to need a lot of them. Budgets are very tight these days." We were told that approval would be requested, but not guaranteed. The consultant said that he would do his best. We left despondent, with me sobbing uncontrollably. I felt sick to the core. I unleashed my rage back in the car in the hospital car park and my husband and I barely spoke all the way home.

Calmed by the silence of the journey, later that day we discussed the future. We both felt that it was looking very bleak indeed. My husband ran his own business, and it wouldn't be possible for him to continue if his sight got worse. We were faced with losing our futures, our dreams and, it has to be said, a large part of our income. How much more could be taken away? I Skyped our 18-year-old daughter, who had taken a gap year and was working as a teacher within the hill tribe area in the North of Thailand. We had been keeping her informed of the deterioration of her dad's eyesight via email. I was becoming increasingly concerned as she never seemed to mention it when replying. I soon found out why. When I pushed her to talk about it, she dropped her head to her hands and sobbed hysterically, alone, thousands of miles away, on the screen in front of me. The body I wanted to hug I just couldn't hold. Later the very same evening I found my husband standing in the garden in the dark, with tears pouring down his face. In a choked whisper, he told me that the stars were beginning to disappear.

Every day my body walked supported by legs detached from my heart, spirit, and soul. It was the only way to survive. My husband and I were both suspended in time and space with a non-existent future. Stuck naked in a lost dimension, with all the 'little life stresses' gone (having paled into insignificance), we found ourselves with an emptiness. It was as if we were floating in space, and the only voices we could hear were our own. In that stillness, and that silence, our souls began to speak.

Our souls told us that we needed to travel, and travel soon. They told us to spend more time enjoying the small things, which are actually the 'really big things'. They said that we should spend more time relaxing, and less time working. They begged us to spend more time outdoors doing the things that we loved. They told us to spend more time talking and walking. They told us spend more time surrounded by sand and water. And they encouraged us to love, and to love more than we had ever loved before. They told us that we were the lucky ones, having been given a very rare gift. It was our reward for getting naked. Suddenly, it all began to make sense. It was the final lesson.

Eight weeks later, guided by our souls, we got onto a plane with backpacks, and headed for Thailand to see our daughter. With our daughter, we travelled from Bangkok on the overnight sleeper towards the beaches in the South. In a rickety old train we lay back in our beds, with open windows, feeling the warm wind against our skin as fireflies danced in the moonlight. We spent the next three days living on a beautiful beach in small wooden huts, drinking from coconuts. We talked, we laughed, and created spectacular family memories. Whilst dining at a tiny restaurant on the shoreline one evening, surrounded by candles in the dark, we even laughed when my husband said that both our daughter's head and a boat floating silently on the sea disappeared when he closed his good eye. And every night we lit sky lanterns, and watched the flames become smaller as they disappeared into the dark velvet night sky.

We then travelled right up through Thailand, stopping off at various towns along the way, joining in with 'Songkran', the water festival, as we went. (The celebrations involve throwing water, everywhere, at everybody for days, from dawn until dusk.) Running around the streets with water pistols and buckets, we joined the locals and whooped with delight. We ate rice, attempted to crunch on crickets, and sampled copious amounts of the most delicious street food releasing mouth-wateringly spectacular aromas, cooked right before our eyes.

Our final few days took us up to the hill tribes in the North, where we stayed in our daughter's teaching accommodation; a remote and very old and minimalistic flat, the kitchen being a gas burner and cold tap on the concrete balcony. There were only two mattresses between five of us, so three slept on the floor. Being Thai school holidays, all other accommodation appeared abandoned, the Thai teachers having returned to their families elsewhere. The only signs of life were the stray dogs that occasionally wandered through. Our family, alone but together, lived with the bare essentials. I've never felt so at home.

At night we would not only hear the songs of many geckos, but the scrabbling of the occasional rat. We witnessed a spectacular two-hour storm one night watching both sheet and forked lightening light up the sky. The thunder was so loud we felt it in our bones. High up in the mountains, living in desolate school grounds in the dark, I have never felt both so scared and so truly alive at the same time. During the day we visited the nearest civilisation, a tiny village called Wawee an hour's walk down the mountain, and spent time amongst the locals who appeared fascinated by the 'strange white people' walking through their streets. We listened to our daughter, whose nose we had once wiped and whose laces we had once tied, introduce us and speak fluent Thai. And it was the best holiday that we have ever, ever had. Pseudoxanthoma Elasticum... thank you.

We returned home, to find to our absolute amazement that the consultant had managed to secure funding for my husband's treatment whilst we had been away. He began having the injections that he so desperately needed, and his eyesight began to improve. To date, he has had many, in both eyes. The injections appear to be working, and have restored most of his sight. His eyes improve but then deteriorate yet again on a regular basis, hence the need for constant medical intervention. Every day we pray that the injections will keep working. His circulation is also badly affected, the majority of his arteries being calcified, and he often suffers with leg pain at night, but is monitored regularly. He now often walks the four miles to work instead of taking the car. This improves his circulation and the chances of him being able to walk properly in later life.

Though my husband's health has improved, we both know that it could get worse at any time, so we live our lives for today. We spend our mid-week day off doing the things that we love together, whether it be walking, having lunch at a favourite café or sitting in our kayaks out at sea, fishing for our supper. We talk more, we laugh more and appreciate every tiny thing that we see, from a blade of grass to the clouds in the sky. I don't have PXE myself but strangely because of it I seem to have a heightened sense of awareness. The trees seem greener, flowers more vibrant, and I notice the beauty of many more smiles. I no longer notice age in people around me, but I do notice their soul and their spirit. And though my husband faces many challenges both now and in the future, he openly and honestly declares that he has never felt happier.

"When it is dark enough, you can see the stars."

Ralph Waldo Emerson

"The naked people looked up, guided by their light. They began to live their lives at a 'higher level', having been enlightened. They lived with more passion and purpose, and sought out adventure. They deepened their connections with other beings, and decided to travel the world, seeking out the beauty of spectacular views. Their knowledge that no one could ever predict the future drove them to live and be the best that they could ever be, today."

The final lesson had been delivered.

CHANGING ROOM TIP

Align With Your Stars

Floating naked in the darkness, seemingly lost in space, everything that doesn't really matter falls away as we notice only the stars. The stars are our values, and they reflect what is truly important to us and the way that we live and work. In the dark night sky, our values shine so bright that they pierce us with their light, enter our bodies, and make a home in our minds forever.

You, the naked one, have millions of stars surrounding you right now, you just need to see them and move towards them. You need to see your stars because by influencing your behaviour, they determine how you live. To be happy, you need to start noticing your twinkles and live your life in alignment with them.

If you value 'family' for example but work an 80-hour week and spend little time with the people that you love, you are highly likely to experience stress. If you value growth, but have been stagnant for years, then you are likely to be unhappy. If your behaviour is incongruent with what is important to you, then you will experience conflict in your mind, which then affects your body. Living your life by someone else's values can be compared to living in amongst someone else's stars. If a shine doesn't belong to you, it won't light you up.

I share with you Melanie's story, to aid your understanding further:

Melanie was a 38-year-old woman with a business degree, working as a personal assistant for a well-known company in London. She worked long hours and had an enviable salary. A breast cancer diagnosis stripped her naked and turned her world upside down overnight, and though she began treatment, the threat of mortality remained in her mind. During long sessions of chemotherapy, she found herself with plenty of time to think, as she began to question the way in which she lived her life. In that time and space, she decided that she was not living a life she had herself planned. A business degree at university had been her parents' choice, and not trusting her own judgement she took their advice. Her parents were wealthy business people, who valued both achievement and security, and wanting the best for their daughter, they had guided her in the only way that they knew.

Melanie began to reflect back, and rediscover her own values. She recalled that as a child and a teenager she had loved being outside. She remembered how alive she felt designing miniature gardens on paper, before creating them within her own family garden at the age of nine. Her thoughts went back to her childhood bedroom wall, covered with pictures of flowers and their proper names. Reminiscing led Melanie to her breakthrough moment. The security of her job wasn't as important to her as she thought. What was important to her was living with passion and being able to unleash her creativity. Following her recovery, Melanie quit her job and pursued a career as a landscape gardener, creating wonderful drawings to excite her customers before transforming their gardens into the picture that they had seen on paper. Melanie, at the age of 38, decided to find her own values, and live amongst her own 'stars'. She took a huge drop in salary, but to this day is adamant that she has never been happier.

Being part of the nudie club, you may already be hearing the messages from your soul, as it tries to reconnect you with your values. Give your soul a helping hand, as you answer the following questions:

What is really important to you in life?

When were you happiest?

What were you doing when you felt most proud?

What makes you feel truly alive?

When did you feel truly fulfilled?

If you only had 10 years left to live, what would you do in those 10 years?

Answering these questions will give huge clues to your values. Below are some of the most common values that I have elicited from my clients over the years:

Achievement, Adventure, Ambition, Belonging, Calm, Challenge, Compassion, Contentment, Connection, Determination, Excitement, Excellence, Faith, Family, Freedom, Growth, Health, Honesty, Hope, Joy, Kindness, Knowledge, Loyalty,

Love, Integrity, Honesty, Passion, Peace, Respect, Recognition, Relaxation, Safety, Security, Solitude, Spirit, Strength, Trust. *(For an extended list and further inspiration, please visit www.mariahocking.com.)*

Use the space below to write down your 8 most important values. What is REALLY important to you in life?

My Most Important Values

☆

☆

☆

☆

☆

☆

☆

☆

Now that you have identified your values, use the space below to put them in order of priority with number 1 being the most important to you. Access your inner wisdom and let your soul be the guide.

My Values In Order Of Importance

1.

2.

3.

4.

5.

6.

7.

8.

Now ask yourself, "Am I living my life in alignment with those values, in that order?" If the answer is "No", then it may well be time to make some changes. To re-dress with happiness, your behaviour must be congruent with your values. It's the difference between existing and living. And life is far too short to just exist.

Knowing your values will give you the ability to make the right decisions about your future. You will only be truly happy when you live your life in accordance with your values. There has never been a better time to discover them. Explore your freedom, and learn to love your birthday suit. You have just been born again.

What action can you take, so that you feel the shine of your own stars and the happiness that they bring?

FINAL WORDS

The once-naked lady emerged from the changing room in a new outfit of her choice and looked in the mirror. She liked what she saw. And she truly appreciated every moment of adversity. Taking a deep breath, with head held high and shoulders back, she stepped smiling into her new life. Having a new sense of time, she began walking determinedly and with purpose. She had a lot of ground to cover in her years left on the earth.

Through my own personal experiences, I have been gifted so much. I know now that the future is totally unpredictable for all of us. We may strive for control, but the truth is anything can happen, at any moment, for any one of us. We can and should plan for the future, but we need to understand that at times, it's necessary to adapt.

The words that I am about to share with you are very personal, and were written as I sat in an elderly care home, with a very special friend who was passing away, in the hours before he took his last breath. At the time I knew that I never wanted to forget what I felt at that moment. Putting pen to paper was a way of making sure that I would always remember. They have been stored away for a few years, and I never intended to share them, but it just feels right to do so, right now.

"I sit listening to the gentle breaths of my dear friend, as he lies peacefully on his bed. A sense of peace fills the room, knowing that his pain is over and that he will soon suffer no more. It's a beautiful sunny day, and an oak tree, encouraged by the gentle warm breeze, brushes its leaves against the window, causing the sunlight to flicker upon the wall. I wonder how many years the tree has stood looking in the window, and I wonder how many souls it has seen, moving from bodies towards the light.

I look at my friend's body, soon to become a 'shell' of what was before, and in this moment I realise that our 'shells' are of such little importance. What really matters is how we 'feel' inside. Nothing else really seems relevant. Our bodies are simply transport for our souls, so that we are able to connect to others in our very short and limited time on earth, before we are taken to another world.

I continue watching his breath, calm but becoming increasingly irregular, and I know it will soon be time for him to leave. I imagine my heart connecting with his and I send as much love as I can, as I close my eyes and try to send a message to his soul.

I hear the delighted screams of small children outside the window; I look down and see tiny naked people sat in a paddling pool. The tiny people sit and play, oblivious that as they play and truly 'live', my friend just metres away is soon to pass through. I sit and send the tiny people love, and hope that they always do what makes their heart sing.

I gaze at my friend, whose breaths are now becoming laboured, and I hold his hand, and I hope he feels my presence. I wonder what goes through his mind in his last few hours. Maybe he thinks of his wife, who lies sleeping in the room next door, just a few bricks away? I hope he too dreams of the microphone that he used to hold, and the songs that he used to sing, and of the people he would 'light up' with his presence. I hope he dreams of his 'magnificent parties' that he used to throw and be so fond of at the famous Halzephron Inn, which brought together the people of the community to sing songs of old. And I know, with absolutely certainty, that nothing else really mattered. And I know that it never will, because in those last few hours, all that isn't worthy of thought, simply falls away. As I look at my friend, I've never been so certain."

My friend who had fought cancer for such a long time taught me two very important lessons: when you get knocked down, never ever stay down, and live every day as if it's your last, because one day it will be.

These learnings combined with my experiences gave me a strong desire to share this message with others. My husband and I learnt that our biggest gift of all was PXE as it made us realise that we need to be living not in 5 years, or 10 years, but today. As a result, we have never been happier. Waiting for the right time to make changes is possible, but it's not reliable. The future is as beautifully unpredictable as the weather at the top of Everest, it can change at any minute without warning for any one of us. And that knowledge is a gift. We need to live for today. YOU need to live for today.

> *"The only things you can take with you when you leave this world are the things you've packed inside your heart."*
>
> Susan Gale

We can't always control what happens to us, but we can control our reactions to our circumstances. Remember that amongst hopelessness and destitution there is always access to a higher life, and this higher life will always be yours for the taking. Within adversity is a gift, the chance to learn to really live, and live the life that you truly deserve.

Getting naked gives us the wonderful and rare opportunity to reconnect with our souls and find our way back to our hearts. Living from our hearts we dazzle with brilliance. Living from our hearts we do what we love. Living from our hearts we shine our light upon others as we light up the world and ourselves. We accept nothing less than being lit up. Only in nakedness do we find our light. Only when we have been stripped of who we thought we were, do we find who we were really meant to be. Only when we've felt nothing, can we become everything. We need to get lost to get found.

Now is your time. It's time to step into your shine. You now have the power to step into the real 'you' because you know the way. Go to who you really are, and your happiness and stand dressed in your best! You need to go for the tiny child that you once were. You need to go for that child who lived with spirit, and for the adult that wants to be that child at heart. Go. Go, knowing that the biggest gift of all is the understanding that you had to get naked.

You always had to get naked to get changed.

Welcome home.

A PERSON WITH GOOD THOUGHTS CANNOT EVER BE UGLY. YOU CAN HAVE A WONKY NOSE AND A CROOKED MOUTH AND A DOUBLE CHIN AND STICK-OUT TEETH, BUT IF YOU ALWAYS HAVE GOOD THOUGHTS THEY WILL SHINE OUT OF YOUR FACE LIKE SUNBEAMS AND YOU WILL ALWAYS LOOK LOVELY.

Roald Dahl

ABOUT THE AUTHOR

UK Life Changer Maria Hocking is an author, inspirational speaker, coach, and motivational trainer. She draws on her own personal life experiences to help others find their light. Her passion for her work simply oozes through her pores, and she is walking talking proof that anyone can change.

Maria spent the early years of her career working in the fitness industry, before developing a deeper interest in emotional health and well-being. Fascinated by the psychology of transformation, she soon developed a thirst for knowledge, and had no choice but to follow her calling. Her own past experiences combined with years of training and endless personal research enable Maria to excel in her field today. She loves nothing more than to change lives with her words and her heart. Maria offers:

- ✓ Inspirational speaking
- ✓ 1-to-1 coaching
- ✓ Group coaching
- ✓ Motivational training (for teachers and students in schools, businesses and organisations)
- ✓ Personal Development workshops
- ✓ 4-hour Breakthrough Sessions

To contact Maria please visit her website: www.mariahocking.com.

At www.mariahocking.com you will also be able to:

- ✓ Download your FREE Changing Room Checklist
- ✓ Download your FREE Happiness Chart (to plot your nakedness and happiness)
- ✓ Subscribe to Maria's newsletter for FREE regular inspiration.
- ✓ Find out more about Maria's motivational events.

UK Life Changer Goes Global

Maria has a huge passion for travel, and has clients worldwide. If you are not based in the UK but are interested in Maria's services then please contact her to discuss your needs. She will travel to most places in the world to help people 'breakthrough' to the life they truly deserve. Tailor-made coaching programmes are offered to suit clients' needs. To find out how she can help YOU, email: info@mariahocking.com.

ACKNOWLEDGEMENTS

This book would not have been possible without the help of so, so many people. Mum and Dad, I'd like to thank you for being there always, to hug and hold and listen. I love you both so much. Your support has been constant and strong, and I wouldn't be the person I am today without you. My biggest learning whilst writing this book was the strength of my family values, which have come from my upbringing. I thank you both with my whole heart. It's without doubt one of the things that I am most proud of. Dad, I love your crazy unpredictable humour, it always brings a huge smile to my face. And I'd like to thank you Mum for not only being you, but for constantly questioning me about the progress of this book. It kept me going more than you will ever know.

Sheila, you are a beautiful person with admirable kindness and compassion. I love how you love to make a difference. John, you have always had the ability to bring a smile to my face and laughter to my cheeks with your endless antics. I'd like to thank you both for always being there, and helping both Paul and myself through the difficult times. Your support too has been unwavering and unconditional.

Paul, I'd like to thank you for your love and support. Amongst baldness and nakedness you have always loved me just as I am, and I love you just as you are. I appreciate you putting up with the restless nights and the endless hours of typing and book talk whilst this all came together. I appreciate all the cups of tea that appeared beside me when I was oblivious to the world around me, lost in my words. As for the way that you deal with a challenging condition, it is truly humbling, and I'm so proud of you.

My children, Jadine, Brook, and Kian, I'm so, so proud of you all, for so many reasons. I love that you all constantly stay true to who you are and I love that you do what you love. And the difference that you all make to others in your own unique ways with your kindness and compassion is truly inspiring. You have all already made your mark on this world, and I know that what you have and continue to offer, the world needs. Your reviews and ideas have helped me so much throughout this whole process. (Though I know I've driven you crazy at times.) I love you all so much x

Martin, my very lovely brother, thank you for always being there. Your words 'sealed the deal' regarding the title of this book, you said exactly what I need to hear. And I love that you are now living your dream. I really love it. You are awesome. Jodie, my equally lovely sister, you inspire me so much, and I love your passion for making a huge difference to the lives of others. I love that you both 'truly live' with your families, and do the things you love. I feel very fortunate to be part of such amazingness.

'Nanny in Norfolk', you continue to inspire me with your zest for life. Accepting nothing less than happiness, you live life to the full. I know that you were very much challenged yourself but you refused to stay down. I love that you have a bigger social life than most people, and that you love adventure. I love that you 'really love your life' and I pray that I will live as you do in my later years.

Shelley, I'd like to thank you for being there through it all. You have always been an incredible friend offering unconditional support. You have the ability to make me feel grounded and calm and have helped me through many difficult times. You are a rock in my life and I would be lost without you. And you are right: tea and cake always make things better.

Trina and Annabel, I truly appreciate your support whilst writing this book. Your early reviews gave me clarity and motivation. You have always been there for me, and you will never know how much you helped me when I found myself bald. You made me smile, laugh, and feel normal when I felt like a freak. Annabel, thank you for your early review, hearing that my words made you laugh and cry gave me motivation to continue. Trina, I feel very lucky to have had my own personal grammar specialist, you helped immensely! Thank you x

Jenny, you are a true friend and my life wouldn't be the same without you. You are always there, and you always make me smile. I was very lucky to have my own 'on call' nurse during my hospital stays, and being able to rant and let off steam when I felt frustrated and incapacitated helped keep me sane. (Almost.)

Sharon, you have been an exceptional friend throughout my life. You have been an incredible support through challenging times, and you always light me up and make me smile. Thank you. You are truly beautiful and I love you x

Wanda, you continue to be a huge inspiration in my life. What you have been through and what you continue to achieve is extraordinary. You really do live your life without limits and you continue to prove to the world that mind-set is everything. You are a true soul mate, and I am very fortunate to have you in my life. You always say what I need to hear. I love you very much. As for your help in the early stages of this book? It gave me huge insight and inspiration. Thank you.

Nick Evans, your training and your ability to deliver such knowledge in such a beautiful way made an incredible difference to my life. I went in a caterpillar and came out a butterfly, with huge and powerful wings. Thank you, for being part of my transformation.

Lizzi Larbalestier, you are awesome. Your ideas, honesty, and guidance as this book came together were exactly what I needed. I love your energy and your #blue mind. Your passion for water and the sea is truly infectious!

Nik and Eva Speakman, you have always been such an inspiration not only to me, but to all of the people who once believed there was no hope. You give hope to so many. What you continue to achieve is nothing short of amazing and I feel privileged to have spent time in your company.

Dr David Hamilton, PhD, training with you has made such a difference to my work and my life. Self-help and science combined are hugely powerful, and the beautiful way in which you deliver your knowledge makes a difference. I take great pride in sharing your knowledge with others, and will continue to do so for the rest of my life. Thank you.

Sue Crew (proprietor of Strawberry Blondes hair salon in Hayle), you will never know what you did for me and how much it meant. You made the outside match the inside of me. Thank you for taking a risk and making a huge difference. It will never be forgotten.

Acknowledgements

Aimee, Lindsey, Deryan, and Deanne, I truly appreciate you allowing me to use your powerful words within this book. I know that your words will give others both knowledge and hope. Thank you so much x

I'd also like to thank every single one of my coaching clients. It has been truly humbling to work with you all. I never tire of your emails informing me of your continuing successes and I feel privileged to have been part of your transformations. You light up my inbox and my life!

And finally, I'd like to give huge thanks to Alison Jones of Practical Inspiration Publishing (www.alisonjones.com) for helping me make this book happen. Thank you for your patience, your clear guidance, and your motivation. I have learnt so much from you throughout this whole process. I could not have done this without you. Your support and advice has been invaluable and exactly what I needed to make my dream come true.